PRAISE FOR
JEWELS FROM MY GROVE

"I have been lucky enough to spend time with Helene Beck, wandering her stunning gardens, exploring the acres of vigorous citrus groves, perusing her massive library of cookbooks, roasting and simmering in her kitchen, and, most memorably, feasting at her table. She made a Fuyu Persimmon and Blood Orange Roulade with Candied Orange Filling (Page 47!) that I will never forget. I cut into citrus and tropical fruits I'd never had before, and my horizons broadened. Visiting Beck Grove was one of the great joys of my life. If you can't make it there, you can still taste Helene's passion through the beautifully crafted recipes in this book."

**Rick Bayless, Chef/Owner of Frontera Grill/Topolobampo/Xoco Chicago
and Host of PBS's "Mexico — One Plate at a Time"**

"Helene Beck is the Goddess of the Grove — dedicating her botanical pursuits to the three most unsung heroes of today's kitchen — kumquats, persimmons, and blood oranges. Thanks to Helene's book *Jewels From My Grove*, this holy trinity of delectable fruits have risen to the prominence they deserve in our home kitchens. The recipes are not only delicious and approachable, but they unlock the mystery of cooking with exotic produce. With every turn of the page you will say, "Wow, I have to make this one!" So, if you want to fall in love with persimmons, make kumquats your new favorite citrus, and vow to add blood oranges to your repertoire, this book is for you!!"

**Ron Oliver, Award-Winning Author
and Chef de Cuisine of The Marine Room**

"For more than 30 years, Helene has been delighting chefs with the most amazing torrent of golden fruit from Beck Grove. We couldn't wait for fall and finally getting to play with the bounty of succulent organic persimmons, kumquats (who doesn't love kumquats?), and astonishing blood oranges. Her original and inventive recipes will send you running to the farmer's market and then to the kitchen!"

**Deborah M. Schneider, Author and Executive Chef/Partner
of SOL Mexican Cocina and solita Tacos & Margaritas**

"In 1994, Helene and Robert Beck converted a neglected avocado ranch in San Diego's fertile North County into a 25-acre grove planted with fifteen different fruit crops. In doing so, they conformed to exacting biodynamic guidelines that view a farm as a living organism. This stunning cookbook is filled with luminous photography as well as mouthwatering recipes that beautifully reflect the results. This is indeed a jewel for your cookbook shelf!"

**Kitty Morse, Author of *Edible Flowers: A Kitchen Companion*
and *The California Farm Cookbook***

"After reading Helene's book, I realize how little many of us may know about these 'mysterious' fruits and how much they have to offer! More than just a cookbook, *Jewels From My Grove* is an informative, compelling, and beautifully illustrated guide to preparing sweet and savory dishes with these amazing fruits. Don't be intimidated...start discovering!"

**Ingrid Croce, Owner of Croce's Park West and
Author of *Photographs and Memories***

Jewels From My Grove
Persimmons, Kumquats & Blood Oranges

Reflections & Recipes

Helene Beck

Photography by Erin Adams and Carl Kravats

Chefs Press, Inc

Copyright © 2015 Chefs Press, Inc. www.chefspress.com

Published by Chefs Press, Inc., San Diego, California
President + Publisher: Amy Stirnkorb
Executive Vice President: Michael D. Pawlenty
Design + Production: Amy Stirnkorb
Editing: Margaret King, Cindy Mushet
Food Stylist + Culinary Consultant: Cindy Epstein

Text copyright: Helene Beck, La Vigne Organics and Beck Grove, www.lavignefruits.com

Photo copyrights:

Erin Adams Photography, www.erinadamsphoto.com
2, 3, 6, 9, 10, 13, 15, 20, 29, 33, 34, 37, 38, 42, 45, 46, 51, 52, 55, 56, 59, 60, 63, 64-65, 67, 68, 71, 72, 75, 85, 90, 94, 97, 98, 101, 105, 109, 100, 114, 118, 121, 125, 126, 129, 133, 134, 137, 138, 141, 142, 145, 146, 150, 154, 157, 158, 161, 165, 166, 176, 182, 197, 198, 201, 202, 206, 209, 213, 214, 217, 218

Carl Kravats Photography, www.carlkravats.com
Cover, 1, 5, 11, 12, 16, 22, 25, 26, 30, 32, 35, 41, 58, 76, 81, 82, 86, 89, 92, 93, 102, 106, 112-113, 122, 128, 136, 152-153, 167, 169, 174, 177, 178, 181, 185, 186, 189, 190, 193, 194, 204, 208, 210, 216, 219, 220, 221, 222

Bruce Jenkins Photography: 130

SPECIAL THANKS:
To Justine Sterling for allowing us to reprint with her permission the excerpt on page 80 from "Consider the Kumquat" originally published in Saveur magazine.

To Leah Koenig for allowing us to reprint with her permission the excerpt on page 172 from "One Ingredient: Many Ways" originally published on Saveur.com.

To The Permissions Company, Inc., on behalf of BOA Editions, Ltd. for allowing us to reprint with permission the excerpt from "Persimmons" by Li-Young Lee on page 18 and the complete poem on page 219.

ISBN: 978-1-939664-00-6
First Edition
Printed in China

To the Love of My Life, Robert —
For a Lifetime of Memories
Rooted in Love, Family, and
the Glories of the Grove

A VERY SPECIAL
THANK YOU

I truly love all the people I worked with
on my book. They were so sincere and
gave their all throughout this long, but
joyous, process. They shared my vision,
and together, we made it happen. This
book is as much theirs as it is mine.

Debbie Hampton

Mark Pequet

Cindy Mushet

Cindy Epstein

Carl Kravats

Erin Adams

Cherisse Holbert

INSIDE

A Short History of Beck Grove

IN 1982, MY HUSBAND, ROBERT, AND I decided to abandon Los Angeles to pursue a more healthful lifestyle. We didn't leave with the intention of starting a grove, but rather stumbled on it while looking for our new home. We had been living in a beautiful, architecturally rich older apartment, but this was not enough to keep us in L.A., especially when the real estate boom brought more people, more noise, and more traffic.

We had lost our tranquility so it was time to move on. Our only requirements were a peaceful environment and being within two hours of our friends in L.A. We were excited when we found an old neglected avocado grove in Fallbrook, a rural agricultural area in the northern part of San Diego County. We were already quite familiar with country living, and loved it. Robert had a cattle ranch in Montana, and we enjoyed splitting our time between L.A.'s city life and the quiet wilds of the Big Sky state.

We were fearless as we embarked upon this new journey. We found the Fallbrook farming community to have a fabulous support system, and when we asked grove manager Mark Pequet to stay on with us, he agreed. Our plan was to bring the avocado grove back to life, rejoining the other successful small farms in the area. This noble goal, however, quickly turned into an educational experience. The trees were failing because of a common root rot, and the methods of saving them offered no guarantee of success.

Given this news, Robert and I decided to start over. Citrus trees were strongly recommended as the best replacement for our soil conditions. So that's what we bought, and

we began replacing the diseased avocado trees with healthy young citrus. All should be fine, right? Well, Mother Nature still had a few more surprises in store for us.

A truck farmer came to us and wanted to grow produce on a portion of our land to sell at markets. This seemed like a good idea at the time, especially since the farmer had a stellar reputation for his crops. But when his cucumbers and tomatoes matured, they were soft and cracked, making them seconds, not the quality produce that commands top dollar. So Robert and I knew we still had problems with our soil.

Fortunately about this time, our neighborhood health food store began featuring all-organic groceries and produce. One day we saw a sign in the store window announcing an organic composting class with Jerry, the store owner, at his farm. We went and were hooked. This marked the turning point for us — we decided we wanted our grove to be like Jerry's farm.

Jerry's farm was all-organic, and he practiced the Demeter method of biodynamic, self-sustaining farming. We could see and taste the difference in his fruits and vegetables, and when he taught classes, we studied with him. We knew organic and sustainable farming was right for us.

Our first step was instituting all-organic principles at our grove. This took three years and required detailed records of everything we did, but we had a goal of rebuilding the soil naturally and creating a sustainable environment. And determined we were!

One of the earliest and most noted proponents of sustainable agriculture was

scientist, philosopher, and educator Dr. Rudolf Steiner (1861-1925). In 1924, he helped a group of European farmers who were concerned with declining crop vitality, animal health, seed quality, and disease resistance. Steiner viewed the farm as a whole organism, a self-sustaining system free of chemicals where the fertility of the soil could be improved through all-natural methods. In order to achieve this, Steiner believed farms must do two things: have their own animals to produce manure for fertilizer and grow their own crops to feed the animals.

So this is what we did. While the journey of working the land to create the proper environment for our trees was long and arduous, it has been well worth it. Now we are a wholly sustainable grove producing fifteen crops of the highest quality, along with having two cows to provide the fertilizer for our grove.

In this book, I want to share my love for my three favorite fruits — persimmons, kumquats, and blood oranges. I have spent more than 30 years growing them and have enjoyed creating nearly 100 wonderful recipes that showcase these luscious and versatile fruits. I hope you will go to your local grocery store or farmer's market and ask for these delicious orange-hued gems so that you will learn to love them as much as I do and will make them your kitchen companions.

About the Author

ROBERT AND I INVESTED A GREAT DEAL OF time and energy in bringing Beck Grove back to prosperity, and throughout it all, our passion never waivered. We love all facets of the grove: the soil, the trees, the landscaping, and the home Robert and I built together. We surrounded our house with all styles and forms of gardens that gently move through the seasons. The wisteria on the back terrace yields to the blooming iris in the fields and in turn to the roses in the white garden, and on and on.

We are also ardent collectors of antiques and old building materials, and we have joyfully incorporated them into our lives and our homes. Our building methods include straw-bale walls and many found treasures. We appreciate the morphing of history — giving new life to once-used items. We filled our log home in Montana with treasures handcrafted by a hardworking rancher who created conveniences and comforts during the long, cold winters. We love the honesty and simplicity of a primitive cabinet or table, so our home is an eclectic mix of these and period pieces.

My interest in food began when I was a young girl. I watched my aunts playfully compete for the honor of best cook and baker with some of their delicious dishes, including kugels, pies, latkes, and rugelachs, while my mother worked hard perfecting her Jell-O combinations and chiffon cakes, both the rage at that time. My grandmother's treats were mostly cookies or yeast breads, though I do remember her making the most luscious, fluffy French toast. Over the years, I too enjoyed the challenge of getting chefs to share their special recipes with me.

Once I learned I could create so many different delicious dishes from a single ingredient, my kitchen creativity blossomed. I studied with an outstanding Chinese culinary instructor who gave me a deep respect for all the efforts of those involved in bringing crops to the market. When we moved to the grove, I learned firsthand what a luxury it is to have fresh produce at my fingertips and to appreciate the hard work of all the people who grow, pick, sort, pack, prepare, and deliver Beck Grove fruit to our customers.

I am as passionate about collecting cookbooks as I am about cooking. I have amassed more than 2,500 cookbooks, and I'm continually on the hunt for new ones to add to my library. Now I have one more, *Jewels From My Grove: Persimmons, Kumquats & Blood Oranges — Reflections and Recipes*. It has always been my dream to have a cookbook of my own so I could share my recipes with you — and that dream has finally come true.

My Gourmet Condiments & Special Recipes

ROBERT AND I STARTED LA VIGNE ORGANICS MORE THAN 20 YEARS AGO IN ORDER to take full advantage of the abundant produce we grow at Beck Grove. We created a delicious line of sauces and condiments, and we also sell our fresh, biodynamic fruit in season directly to customers at www.lavignefruits.com.

To prepare dishes from this book, you will need to have fresh seasonal fruit on hand along with a number of the sauces. Maybe you have your own fruit trees. If not, check your local grocery store or farmer's market, and if they don't carry the fruits, see if they can order what you want. Ask your grocer to call us at (760) 723-9997 or Specialty Produce in Southern California at (619) 295-3172.

You can purchase the condiments and sauces pre-made from our website or can you make them with the recipes I share on the following pages. Enjoy!

Fuyu Persimmon Purée

Select any number of ripe Fuyu persimmons. Test for ripeness by giving the flesh a soft squeeze, as you would an avocado. It should yield to moderate pressure. Remove the calyx (flower-like top) and cut each persimmon into pieces. You don't need to peel the fruit. Purée in a food processor, scraping the sides frequently, until the fruit turns to a thick liquid. Transfer to an airtight container and refrigerate. Use within 3 days. It also freezes well and will keep up to 1 year. Best to freeze in 1-cup portions.

How to Dry Fuyu Persimmons

Select firm Fuyu fruit, when the skin is a rich orange, remove any stems and leaves, and slice horizontally into circles. Place in a dehydrator or oven at 140°F until the fruit disks are dry and pliable with no moist areas. The time needed to dry the fruit depends on a number of factors: the size of the slices, the humidity level, and the air circulation in the dehydrator. Drying will take more than 8 hours. Transfer to an airtight container. When properly prepared, dried fruit will keep for 6 to 12 months.

Fuyu Persimmon Salsa

Makes approximately 2½ cups

2 Fuyu persimmons, diced into ¼-inch pieces
½ medium yellow onion, diced into ¼-inch pieces
¾ cup lightly packed chopped fresh cilantro leaves
¼ cup water
¼ cup fresh apple juice
½ cup fresh lemon juice
2 tablespoons apple cider vinegar
⅛ teaspoon salt
⅛ teaspoon white pepper
¼ teaspoon seeded and minced fresh jalapeño or other pepper, or to taste

In a bowl, mix all ingredients well. Transfer to an airtight container and refrigerate to let flavors meld. Use within 7 days.

Fuyu Persimmon Chipotle Sauce

Makes approximately 3½ cups

2 cups Fuyu Persimmon Purée (above)
1 cup fresh orange juice
½ cup apple cider vinegar
2 tablespoons light brown sugar
2 tablespoons fresh lime juice
2 tablespoons peeled and grated fresh ginger
¼ cup grated yellow onion
3 cloves roasted garlic, smashed into a paste
1 teaspoon salt
¼ teaspoon white pepper
1 teaspoon mashed, puréed, or ground chipotle chile or chipotle chili powder

Mix all ingredients in a saucepan, bring to a boil, and let boil for 1 minute. Remove from heat and cool in pan. Transfer to an airtight container and refrigerate. Use within 7 days.

Kumquat Purée

Select any number of ripe kumquats. Purée in a food processor, scraping the sides frequently, until the fruit turns to a fine liquid. Transfer purée to an airtight container and refrigerate. Use within 3 days. It also freezes well and will keep up to 1 year. Best to freeze in 1-cup portions.

Kumquat Conserve

Makes approximately 2 to 2½ cups

Note: *I use Kumquat Conserve in a variety of ways throughout this book. In some dishes, I use the Conserve just as it comes in the jar commercially prepared or as made following this recipe. In other dishes, I use only the kumquat halves, either as an ingredient or as a pretty decoration. Depending upon how sweet you wish the finished appetizer, entrée, or dessert to be, you may want to rinse the kumquat halves before using them in order to remove the thin coating of sugary syrup on the pieces. You may also want to rinse and dry them if you need flour to adhere to the pieces. And always be sure to check for any stray seeds before using the Conserve.*

1 pound fresh kumquats
2 cups granulated sugar
1 cup water

Cut kumquats in half and remove seeds. Set aside. Bring sugar and water to a boil, and then lower the heat and simmer for about 10 minutes. Drop kumquats into the simmering syrup and cook until tender, about 30 minutes. Let cool slightly. Transfer to an airtight container and refrigerate. Use within 3 months.

Kumquat Piquant Sauce

Makes approximately 2 cups

1 cup seeded and chopped fresh kumquats (measure after chopping)
½ cup peeled, seeded, and chopped apples (measure after chopping)
1 tablespoon orange or Blood Orange Marmalade (page 15)
2 tablespoons pineapple juice
1 tablespoon unsweetened frozen orange juice concentrate
½ cup granulated sugar
1 tablespoon finely grated fresh ginger
2 teaspoons apple cider vinegar
¼ teaspoon crushed dried chili peppers

Combine all ingredients in a medium saucepan and simmer for 20 to 30 minutes. Cool. Transfer to an airtight container and refrigerate. Use within 2 weeks.

Kumquat Ginger Syrup

Makes approximately 1 to 1¼ cups

1 cup Kumquat Purée (above)
1 cup water
1 cup granulated sugar
2 teaspoons peeled and grated fresh ginger

In a saucepan, bring purée, water, sugar, and ginger to a boil. Lower heat and simmer for 15 minutes. Set a clean fine-mesh strainer over a bowl and pour the mixture into the strainer, pressing out as much liquid as possible. Discard solids. You should have about 1¼ cups liquid or syrup remaining. Let cool slightly. Transfer to an airtight container and refrigerate. Use within 3 months.

BLOOD ORANGE MARMALADE

Makes approximately 6 cups

4 blood oranges (about 1½ pounds)
1 large Meyer lemon
8 cups water
7 cups granulated sugar

Using a channel knife to make thin strips, remove the peel from the blood oranges and lemon. Cut the fruit in half, squeeze out the juice and place any seeds in a cheesecloth bag. Pour the juice into large, heavy saucepan. Add seeds, peel, and water, stirring to combine. Bring to a boil, reduce heat to low, and simmer for 1½ hours, stirring occasionally, until peel is very tender, and the sauce is thickened and not too runny. Stir in sugar and bring to boil over high heat for about 10 minutes, stirring constantly, until set. To test, place a teaspoonful on a cold plate. The surface should gel and a fork drawn through it should create wrinkles.

Pour mixture into 6 (1 cup) hot sterilized canning jars, leaving ¼-inch headspace. Cover with new sterilized lids and screw on outer ring without forcing.

Process filled jars in a boiling water bath. Bring a large stockpot filled with water to a boil. Add jars (in batches, if necessary), cover, bring back to boil, and boil for 5 minutes. Remove the jars from the water and place on racks to cool. Listen for the "ping" from the jars; it's the lids locking down to announce that a perfect seal has been made. Wipe jars, label, and store in cool, dark, and dry place. If any jars do not seal, simply refrigerate and use within 3 months.

PERSIMMONS

PERSIMMONS

Excerpt from the poem "Persimmons" by Li-Young Lee.
Reprinted with permission of The Permissions Company, Inc., on behalf of BOA Editions, Ltd.

In sixth grade Mrs. Walker
slapped the back of my head
and made me stand in the corner
for not knowing the difference
between persimmon and precision.
How to choose

persimmons. This is precision.
Ripe ones are soft and brown-spotted.
Sniff the bottoms. The sweet one
will be fragrant. How to eat:
put the knife away, lay down newspaper.
Peel the skin tenderly, not to tear the meat.
Chew the skin, suck it,
and swallow. Now, eat
the meat of the fruit,
so sweet,
all of it, to the heart. . . .

Mrs. Walker brought a persimmon to class
and cut it up
so everyone could taste
a Chinese apple. Knowing
it wasn't ripe or sweet, I didn't eat
but watched the other faces.

My mother said every persimmon has a sun
inside, something golden, glowing,
warm as my face.

The full version of this beautiful poem is included in the Appendix.
It's worth taking the time to read. It is really quite enchanting.

Persimmons: Fruit of the Gods

IN MANY CULTURES AROUND THE WORLD, especially in Asia, persimmons are a valued and prized fruit. But in the United States, the poor little persimmon is sadly misunderstood, and many people have no idea how to eat it or cook with it. So in this chapter, I am going to stand on my "persimmon soapbox" and declare its virtues through a little history, some tasty tidbits, and more than 25 savory and sweet recipes for you to explore.

Robert and I chose to plant persimmons at Beck Grove for a number of reasons: hardiness, resistance to disease and pests, sturdiness (they're part of the ebony tree family), and adaptability to a wide range of climates. They are deciduous trees, grow swiftly, and have a strong root system, making them ideal for helping to recover habitat. Persimmons helped us heal our land.

Persimmons are a wonderful fruit, about the size and shape of a medium tomato. They are somewhat squat, ranging in color from a deep reddish orange to a vivid golden orange hue, with a flower-like top or stem called a calyx. The fruit is generally harvested between mid- to late October and December (that's when we pick our persimmons), but specific timing depends upon growing location.

There are two types of persimmons — astringent and non-astringent — and each has a very different taste if eaten before fully ripened. This may be one reason why the persimmon is not an everyday fruit in the U.S. Two common astringent persimmons are the Native American and Asian Hachiya, which both have a most unpleasant tannic flavor if eaten before fully ripened. Your tongue feels like sandpaper and the inside of your mouth like a dried up beach towel, and worse, they'll stay that way for a few minutes! But once an astringent persimmon is fully ripened and its flesh soft enough to spoon, its flavor turns light and sweet.

Now, if you bite into a non-astringent persimmon, such as a Fuyu, it may immediately become one of your favorite fruits because it can be enjoyed when it is firm to the touch yet gives gently in the palm of your hand, like a ripe avocado. I eat them like an apple, just as many Asian cultures do, by simply biting into the somewhat crunchy flesh. As they ripen, their sweetness intensifies and they become softer, similar to a soft peach. Fuyus are by far the most popular and well-known persimmon worldwide.

The taste of a ripe persimmon is hard to describe — because a persimmon tastes like a persimmon and nothing else! The persimmon has a unique sweetness that is very delicate and luscious. Even more than 400 years ago, Thomas Hariot, a scientist in the second Roanoke expedition to the New World in 1585, similarly described the permission: "As red as cherries and very sweet: but whereas the cherrie is sharpe and sweet, they are lushious sweet." He clearly tasted a very ripe Native American persimmon.

All persimmons are part of the genus *Diospyros*, which means "fire of Zeus" in ancient Greek. The name likely was loosely translated into "fruit of Zeus" or "pear of Zeus," which is where the phrase "fruit of the gods" probably originated. Many persimmons are natives of China, where they were cultivated for centuries, but they spread to Japan and Southeast Asia. In the 1800s, the Japanese

persimmon was introduced to California, and since then a number of varieties have been developed from it.

The Fuyu (*Diospyros kaki*) is one persimmon that originated in China but was cultivated and popularized by the Japanese, who named it "Fuyu," after the Japanese word *Fuyugaki*, meaning "winter persimmon." The Fuyu thrives best in sub-tropical climates, including Florida, California, and Texas.

Native American persimmon trees (*Diospyros virginiana*) have grown naturally throughout most of the United States for hundreds of years, and during chilly, gray fall and winter days, Native American persimmons are a welcome sight — their beautiful orange fruit still hanging on leafless branches. It was the Native American persimmon that Captain John Smith (1580-1631) described growing in Virginia on his visit to the New World: "If it be not ripe it will drawe a man's mouth awrie with much torment: but when it is ripe, it is as delicious as an apricock."

The American Indians knew all about persimmons and incorporated this highly nutritious fruit into their daily diet. The word "persimmon" is derived from putchamin, pasiminan, or pessamin, which in the Algonquian language means "a dry fruit." They dried them, shaped them into loaves, and ate them. They also used the persimmons as a sweetener in cornbread, fermented the fruit with honey locust pods to create an alcoholic brew, and dried and ground the seeds into flour.

To best enjoy the astringent Native American and Asian Hachiya (*Diospyros kaki*) persimmons, they must be over-ripened,

Air drying persimmons, above, and donut-like dried persimmons, below.

or bletted, before eating. During the bletting process, tannins are naturally eliminated, which allows the flesh to soften and the sugar content to increase. Native persimmons should not be picked, but allowed to ripen until they fall from the tree. Hachiyas can be picked and then forced to ripen by placing them in a clean, dry container along with other fruits such as apples or pears that naturally release ethylene gas while they ripen, which will jumpstart the persimmons' ripening process.

Because of their growing season from fall to winter, persimmons often appear in Thanksgiving dishes and other traditional recipes, such as baked puddings, pies, syrups, jellies, and jams, but they really are much more versatile. They can be peeled and air-dried, and are ready to eat when they flatten and look like donuts dusted in powdered sugar. This way, they become quite sweet, chewy, and delicious, and are also an excellent source of dietary fiber and vitamin C. I prefer to dry Fuyus (see page 13) but all varieties are delicious dried and are considered a delicacy in many parts of the world.

I love Fuyu persimmons the best — that's what I prefer to grow, and that's what I cook with, but feel free to try other varieties available to you. Cooking with them for more than 20 years has given me the opportunity to use both fresh and dried persimmons to enhance or star in hundreds of sweet and savory dishes I created. I am sharing with you my favorite recipes with the hope that the Fuyu persimmon will become as loved in your home as it is in mine.

Cool Palate-Pleasing Fuyu Persimmon and Blood Orange Soup

Because Fuyu persimmons maintain their flavor even when frozen, you can enjoy them year-round. This soup also works as a fabulous dessert. Just pour into martini glasses and serve with Madeleines or crisp butter cookies. I promise, your guests will remember it!

Serves 4

In a small bowl, combine ginger, nutmeg, and 2 tablespoons orange juice to make a paste. Place Fuyu persimmons in a blender or food processor and pulse until creamy and smooth. Add ginger paste and remaining ingredients, and process until well combined. Transfer to an airtight container and refrigerate.

Serve chilled. I also love this with a dash of freshly ground nutmeg. As a dessert, top with a dollop of whipped cream or crème fraîche and swirl into soup.

1 teaspoon fresh or ground ginger

½ teaspoon freshly ground nutmeg

1 cup blood orange juice, divided

3 or 4 fresh Fuyu persimmons, calyx removed and cut into quarters

½ cup granulated sugar, or to taste

½ teaspoon salt, if desired

¼ cup good-quality bourbon or brandy

¾ cup half-and-half

Finishing Touches

Freshly ground nutmeg

Homemade whipped cream or crème fraîche

CHIPOTLE FUYU PERSIMMON AND PUMPKIN SOUP

Fuyu persimmons and pumpkins are in season in the fall when the weather begins to have a chill in the air. Even here at Beck Grove in Southern California, 18 miles away from the Pacific Ocean, we actually enjoy four seasons. In fact, it's the cool nights and warm days that contribute to the excellent quality and flavor of our fruit.

Serves 8 to 10

1 (8- to 10-pound) fresh pumpkin or 6 cups canned unsweetened pumpkin

3 tablespoons salted butter

1 large yellow onion, diced

8 cups vegetable or chicken stock

2½ cups Fuyu Persimmon Chipotle Sauce (page 13)

1 cup half-and-half

Salt and freshly ground black pepper

Finishing Touches

Fuyu Persimmon Chipotle Sauce (page 13)

Crème fraîche

Fresh chives

Preheat oven to 375°F and position a rack in the center of the oven.

To use fresh pumpkin, cut it in half or quarters, remove the seeds, and bake, cut side down, for about 45 minutes, or until soft. Remove the skin and purée the flesh in a blender until smooth and creamy.

Melt butter in a stockpot over medium-low heat and add onions. Cook for 7 to 10 minutes, stirring occasionally, until onions become translucent. Add fresh pumpkin purée or canned pumpkin, stock, and a pinch of salt. Increase heat to medium-high. Stir in Fuyu Persimmon Chipotle Sauce. Add half-and-half and stir. Remove from heat and purée in batches, being careful to never fill the blender more than halfway. Adjust seasoning with salt and pepper.

Garnish with more Fuyu Persimmon Chipotle Sauce, crème fraîche, and chives. Or, transfer to an airtight container, refrigerate, and use within 3 days. To reheat soup, gently warm over medium-low heat.

ABOUT CHIPOTLE PEPPERS

Chipotles are actually smoked jalapeño peppers. They impart a smoky, earthy spiciness and are often used in salsas, sauces, and slow-cooked dishes such as soups and stews.

The jalapeños are not harvested until they turn a very dark red and lose most of their moisture. Then they are placed in special smokers for several days and stirred often, so the smoke penetrates them. The last step in the process is for the peppers to be browned and dried. They are then packaged as is, ground into a powder, or canned as chipotle in adobo, which is a lightly seasoned sauce made with vinegar and paprika.

Adobo is a Spanish word meaning marinade, sauce, or seasoning. Adobo was originally used to preserve raw food because the vinegar and paprika have antibacterial properties, but now it is a popular condiment.

Southwest Fuyu Persimmon and Roasted Red Pepper Soup

This sweet and smoky soup makes a great first course for any meal. Serve it with my Blood Orange Salad with Candied Almonds on page 175 for a light supper. Add your favorite crusty bread or a hearty cornbread, and dinner's on the table.

Serves 4 to 6

If using fresh bell peppers, preheat broiler and position a rack about 4 inches away from heat. Place peppers on a lightly oiled sheet pan, and broil, turning frequently, for about 5 to 8 minutes, or until charred on all sides. When done, place peppers in a plastic or brown paper bag. Close bag and let stand for 15 minutes to let steam loosen the skin. Trim off stems, strip off skins, remove seeds and veins and discard.

Coarsely chop freshly roasted or store-bought peppers and pulse in a blender or food processor until smooth. Set aside.

In a 3-quart saucepan over medium heat, melt butter and add flour, stirring constantly to prevent lumps. Stir in half-and-half or light cream and broth, and bring to a boil. Immediately reduce heat and simmer for 2 minutes. Stir in puréed peppers and Fuyu Persimmon Chipotle Sauce. Heat through. Season with salt and pepper.

Serve hot with crusty bread or cool to room temperature then transfer to an airtight container and refrigerate. Soup will thicken upon chilling. Gently reheat over medium-low and add a little milk or light cream to the soup, if needed.

3 fresh red bell peppers or 1½ cups store-bought roasted red peppers

3 tablespoons salted butter

3 tablespoons unbleached all-purpose flour

2 cups half-and-half or light cream

1 cup chicken broth

¾ cup Fuyu Persimmon Chipotle Sauce, or to taste (page 13)

Salt and freshly ground black pepper, to taste

MAHI-MAHI QUESADILLA
WITH FUYU PERSIMMON SALSA

In Southern California excellent Mexican food abounds, and fresh fish is often used in tacos, burritos, and quesadillas. This is one of my favorite quesadillas to make. I'm pretty sure no one else is serving Fuyu Persimmon Salsa with their fish tacos...yet!

Serves 4 to 8

4 tablespoons vegetable oil

1½ pounds fresh Mahi-Mahi or your favorite fish fillets

Salt and freshly ground black pepper, to taste

8 (8- to 9-inch or burrito-size) flour tortillas

1 cup grated white cheddar cheese

¾ cup grated Tetilla or other easy melting cheese (such as mild cheddar or Jack)

⅓ cup finely diced water chestnuts

⅓ cup chopped fresh chives

Finishing Touches

Chopped fresh parsley

1 cup Fuyu Persimmon Salsa (page 13)

To prepare the Mahi-Mahi, heat 2 tablespoons oil in large skillet over medium-high heat. You will likely have to cook the fish in batches. When the pan is hot, add the fillets, being careful not to overcrowd the pan. Depending on the thickness of the fish, cook for 3 to 5 minutes on one side, turn, and cook another 3 to 5 minutes until the flesh easily flakes with a fork. Repeat with remaining fillets. When fish is cool, flake into bite sized chunks and set aside.

Using the same skillet, wipe away all the oil and reduce heat to medium or medium-low. Place a tortilla in the pan and layer with one-quarter of the fish, cheeses, water chestnuts, and chives. Cover with another tortilla. Lightly brown both sides to melt cheese. Slide onto a cutting board and cut into 6 triangles. Repeat for remaining quesadillas.

Plate and garnish with parsley leaves and Fuyu Persimmon Salsa.

ABOUT TETILLA CHEESE

Tetilla is a mild, soft, buttery cow's milk cheese from the Galician area of northern Spain. It is creamy and slightly salty, with a fine texture and ivory color. In Galician, tetilla means "small breast." The name describes the unique shape of this cheese.

Fuyu Persimmon Chipotle Risotto with Scallops

Robert and I love the creamy texture and taste of risotto, so I came up with an imaginative way to serve it. I first tried the recipe with scallops, and over the years, I found it also works very well with shrimp or veal. Adding Parmesan cheese mellows the flavor.

Serves 4 to 6

In a blender or food processor, purée 1 cup corn and set aside. In a 3-quart saucepan over medium heat, melt butter and sauté remaining corn with onions and carrots for 3 minutes. Stir in the Arborio rice and sauté for 2 minutes. Add wine and cook, stirring constantly, until liquid is fully absorbed.

To the rice and vegetables, add enough broth to cover and stir frequently until liquid is fully absorbed. Repeat until all of the broth is used except for 2 tablespoons of broth for later use.

Stir in the Fuyu Persimmon Chipotle Sauce and cook, stirring frequently, for 10 minutes more, or until liquid is absorbed and rice is tender. If rice needs to cook longer, add the 2 tablespoons of reserved broth and continue stirring until tender. Total cooking time should be 25 to 30 minutes. Stir in scallops, corn purée, and Parmesan cheese. Cook 2 minutes more, or until scallops are opaque and mixture is heated through. For added crunch and color, serve with quickly blanched pea pods, if desired.

Variations: *For shrimp risotto, replace scallops with shrimp and cook until pink and opaque. For veal risotto, pan-fry until done as desired. Add to risotto, stir in corn purée and Parmesan cheese, and cook until heated through.*

1½ cups fresh or frozen and thawed corn, divided

¼ cup salted butter

½ cup diced red onion

½ cup diced carrots

⅔ cup Arborio rice

¼ cup dry white wine

2 cups chicken broth, divided

1 cup Fuyu Persimmon Chipotle Sauce (page 13)

1 pound fresh or frozen and thawed bay scallops

¼ cup grated Parmesan cheese

Finishing Touch

1 cup pea pods, quickly blanched, and cut in half diagonally, if desired

Variations

1 pound medium peeled and deveined shrimp

1 pound thinly sliced veal cutlets

ABOUT ARBORIO RICE

Risotto is an Italian dish made with Arborio rice, a variety of short-grain rice with a high starch content. It is this starchy quality that brings the creaminess to risotto dishes. Although there are several varieties of Italian rice used to make risotto, Arborio is the most common. Rice began its journey to Italy from China and the Far East, where it has been cultivated since about 6000 BC. Then during the seventh and eighth centuries, Arabs were believed to have brought rice to Spain, Sicily, and the Po Valley in northern Italy, where the climate is humid and wet. The flat valley makes it perfect for rice cultivation.

FUYU PERSIMMON SPICED SHRIMP NOODLES

This is my go-to recipe when I have no time to cook. Most of us have these simple ingredients in our kitchens. No snow peas? Substitute broccoli florets or mushrooms. No shrimp? Reach for chicken. There are really no rules with this quick and easy dish except to enjoy it!

Serves 4

2 to 3 tablespoons peanut oil

1 cup peeled and julienned carrots

½ cup sliced yellow onion

2 cloves garlic, minced

1 cup snow peas, cut in half diagonally

2 cups julienned cucumber

1¼ pounds peeled and deveined large shrimp

4 ounces cooked and drained dried vermicelli

1½ cups Fuyu Persimmon Salsa (page 13)

In a large wok or skillet, heat 1 tablespoon oil over high heat. Sauté carrots, onion, and garlic for 3 minutes, or until vegetables are crisp-tender. Remove from wok. Add more oil if necessary. Stir-fry snow peas for 2 minutes. Add cucumbers for the last 30 second and toss. Remove from wok.

Add more oil to the wok if necessary. Stir-fry shrimp until pink and opaque. Add noodles and toss for 2 minutes. Add Fuyu Persimmon Salsa and cooked vegetables. Toss together well and cook 2 more minutes, or until heated through.

Serve immediately.

GRILLED LOBSTER
WITH FUYU PERSIMMON CHIPOTLE SAUCE

For a special barbecue, try these luscious lobsters! Add steak to the menu and you'll turn any dinner into a memorable surf-and-turf alfresco party. Serve with a citrus rice pilaf and a mixed green salad, and you've got a great meal with very little effort.

Serves 4

Preheat a gas grill to medium-high, or for charcoal, distribute the hot coals evenly. Clean and oil grates prior to cooking. If using bamboo skewers, soak them in water for at least 2 hours before using to prevent burning.

Place each lobster tail on its back on a work surface and use kitchen shears to make a vertical cut along the soft underside of the shell down to the tail.

Thread a skewer lengthwise through the flesh of each lobster to prevent the tail from curling. Mix oil or butter and lime juice, and baste each lobster with the mixture.

Grill lobsters flesh side down for 4 to 5 minutes, until light grill marks show. Turn and cook shell side down for 3 to 6 minutes, until the lobster meat is firm and opaque. Continue to baste with lime mixture while cooking. Remove from heat and let rest for a few minutes.

Serve lobster hot with Fuyu Persimmon Chipotle Sauce on the side. Delicious with your favorite corn salad and a squeeze of lime, if desired.

4 (8- to 10-ounce) fresh or frozen (and thawed) lobster tails, shell on

3 to 4 tablespoons vegetable oil or melted salted butter

1 tablespoon fresh lime juice

Finishing Touches

½ cup Fuyu Persimmon Chipotle Sauce (page 13)

Corn salad, if desired

Lime wedges, if desired

FUYU PERSIMMON CHINESE CHICKEN WITH CRISPY RICE STICKS AND PLUM SAUCE

Chinese rice sticks, sometimes called rice noodles, create a perfect nest for this dish. If you haven't had these before, you're in for a real treat! They get puffy and crunchy when quickly cooked in hot oil. Top them with my persimmon chicken and you have a delightful mixture of sweet and savory flavors along with contrasting textures and a beautiful presentation.

Serves 4 to 6

Plum Sauce

⅓ cup rice vinegar

½ cup granulated sugar

2 teaspoons salt

1 pitted sweet plum, chopped

1 tablespoon spicy chili or Sriracha sauce

Quick Plum Sauce

¾ to 1 cup bottled plum sauce

2 tablespoons blood orange juice

½ teaspoon bottled sweet chili sauce

Rice Sticks

4 ounces dry rice sticks

2 cups peanut oil

Stir-Fry

3 boneless skinless chicken breast halves, cubed

1 egg white, lightly beaten

¼ to ⅓ cup cornstarch

½ cup diced green onions

1 tablespoon peeled and grated fresh ginger

1 cup diced Fuyu persimmons

½ cup sliced water chestnuts

Finishing Touches

4 to 6 cups mixed greens

Chopped fresh cilantro

Note: *The bottled plum sauce, spicy chili or Sriracha sauce, sweet chili sauce, rice sticks, and water chestnuts can be found in well-stocked grocery stores and Asian markets. I'm giving you two recipes to choose from for the plum sauce — a scratch-made and a quick version using bottled sauce.*

To make the from-scratch plum sauce, place all ingredients in a saucepan and gently simmer over medium heat until sugar dissolves. As you stir, smash and break apart the plum to get the full flavor. Set aside.

To make the quick plum sauce, mix bottled plum sauce, blood orange juice, and bottled sweet chili sauce. Set aside.

To make the rice sticks, separate sticks into 4 to 6 sections, depending upon number of servings. Heat oil in a wok over medium-high. To test the oil temperature, drop a small piece into the oil, and when it puffs up, the oil is ready. Drop bundles into the oil in batches, cooking for 5 to 10 seconds. When done, remove and place on paper towels to drain.

To stir-fry the chicken, drain all but about 2 tablespoons oil from the wok and reheat on medium-high. Dip chicken in egg whites, lightly dust with cornstarch, add to hot oil and stir-fry for 2 minutes, or until thoroughly cooked. Remove chicken and set aside. Next stir-fry onions and ginger for 1 minute, or until soft. Add persimmons, water chestnuts, ¼ cup plum sauce, and cooked chicken. Stir-fry for 2 more minutes. Remove from heat.

To serve, build a bed of salad greens, rice sticks, stir-fried chicken and sauce, and a sprinkling of cilantro. Serve remaining plum sauce on the side, if desired.

PORTUGUESE FUYU PERSIMMON CHICKEN

*There must be as many variations on Portuguese chicken as there are cooks
who make it. Traditionally, this dish features piri piri or bird's-eye chiles and rich earthy spices.
My version features Fuyu Persimmon Salsa — which gets its peppery kick from jalapeños
— along with a fragrant blend of herbs and spices to create a distinctive flavor. This dish is
particularly good the next day, after the seasonings have melded.*

Serves 4

For the marinade, grind cumin seed, mustard seed, and fennel seed in a mini food processor or coffee grinder. Add ginger and remaining seasonings, and pulse until well combined. Pour spice mixture into a bowl and stir in Fuyu Persimmon Salsa. Set aside.

To prepare the chicken, arrange breasts in a non-aluminum dish and pour the marinade over top. Cover and refrigerate for 30 minutes, or up to 24 hours.

When ready to cook, drain marinade and reserve. Heat oil in a large skillet over medium-high heat and brown chicken on both sides. Transfer chicken to a plate, pour marinade into the skillet and bring to a boil. Reduce heat, return chicken to the pan and simmer for 15 minutes, or until chicken is no longer pink in the center.

Serve chicken and sauce over couscous, rice, quinoa, or rice noodles.

Marinade

2 teaspoons cumin seed

**2 teaspoons black or yellow
mustard seed**

½ teaspoon fennel seed

**1 tablespoon peeled and
grated fresh ginger**

1 teaspoon ground turmeric

1 teaspoon ground cinnamon

**¼ teaspoon ground
cardamom**

**1 cup Fuyu Persimmon Salsa
(page 13)**

Chicken

**4 boneless skinless chicken
breast halves**

1 to 2 tablespoons olive oil

Fuyu Persimmon Pork Tenderloin with Carrots and Green Onions

This is one of my favorite recipes for pork. It's easy and requires very little preparation. Persimmons originated in China, and this recipe combines them with soy sauce, sesame seeds, and cilantro, bringing together traditional Asian flavors with an unexpected twist. And although chipotle is not a traditional flavor used in Asian cooking, chile peppers have been an important part of Asian cuisine for centuries.

Serves 4 to 6

1 (1- to 1½-pound) pork tenderloin, cut into 1½-inch slices

2 to 4 tablespoons vegetable oil, divided

½ cup Fuyu Persimmon Chipotle Sauce (page 13)

6 peeled carrots, cut into ½-inch diagonal pieces

2 bunches green onions, cut into 1-inch diagonal pieces

1 tablespoon light soy sauce

1 teaspoon granulated sugar

3 tablespoons white sesame seeds, toasted if desired

Preheat broiler.

In a large oven-safe skillet over medium-high heat, sear pork slices in 1 to 2 tablespoons oil. Brush with Fuyu Persimmon Chipotle Sauce and place under the broiler to caramelize sauce. Watch closely so meat doesn't burn. Carefully remove the pan from oven and cover with foil.

Heat remaining oil in another sauté pan over high heat. Add carrots and cook for about 2 minutes. Add green onions and cook for about 1 minute more. Stir in soy sauce and sugar. Cook for 30 seconds more.

To serve, plate pork slices, sprinkle with sesame seeds, and drizzle sauce over the top. Serve with carrots and green onions along with your favorite rice.

Fuyu Persimmon Chipotle Prime Rib with Cardamom Spice Rub

A beautifully prepared prime rib roast has come to signify holiday family dinners. This is the time when I avoid overly complicated recipes and stick with classic dishes. But I always need to add a little surprise — a fancy garnish, a unique ingredient — something to mark the occasion, and persimmons are in season for the holidays! Here's a new spin on an old favorite.

Serves 8

Preheat oven to 450°F and position a rack in the center of the oven.

To make the spice rub, combine garlic, salt, ground ginger, ground cardamom, and black pepper. Set aside.

To prepare the meat, first make incisions between the bones of the rib roast, open pockets, and rub with spice mixture. Place in a roasting pan and baste with olive oil. Cook for 15 minutes, then lower heat to 325°F. Cook until an instant-read thermometer registers an internal temperature of 120°F to 125°F for rare. About 5 minutes before end of cooking time, baste the beef with Fuyu Persimmon Chipotle Sauce.

Serve with slices of Dried Fuyu Persimmons, if desired.

4 garlic cloves, minced or crushed

Salt, about 1 teaspoon per rib, or as desired

2 teaspoons ground ginger

1 teaspoon ground cardamom

2 teaspoons freshly ground black pepper

1 (8-pound) beef prime rib roast

Olive oil, as needed

1 cup Fuyu Persimmon Chipotle Sauce (page 13)

Dried Fuyu Persimmons, if desired (page 13)

43

ABOUT PRIME RIB

Prime rib is traditionally served juicy and rare. Rare beef is cooked to an internal temperature of 120°F to 125°F with a bright-red center that grows slightly pinkish toward the exterior. Cooking times will vary depending on the size of the roast and desired level of doneness. The table below shows approximate roasting times.

Number of ribs	Prime rib weight in pounds	Time in minutes	Temperature in °F	Time in hours	Temperature in °F
3	7 - 8	15	450	1¼ - 1½	325
4	9 - 10	15	450	1½ - 2	325
5	11 - 13	15	450	2 - 2½	325
6	14 - 16	15	450	2¾ - 3	325
7	16 - 18	15	450	3 - 3¾	325

FUYU PERSIMMON GINGERBREAD BUNDT CAKE

*This cake is especially welcome in the fall season when Fuyu persimmons are ripe.
It is an easy-to-bake scratch cake that is as comfortable next to the pumpkin pie on the
Thanksgiving table as it is with a cup of tea for a midafternoon snack.*

Makes 1

Batter

**1½ sticks unsalted butter,
room temperature**

**¾ cup packed light brown
sugar**

¾ cup pure maple syrup

**3 large eggs, room
temperature**

**1 teaspoon pure vanilla
extract**

**1½ cups plus 3 tablespoons
Fuyu Persimmon Purée
(page 13)**

**2⅔ cups unbleached
all-purpose flour**

1 tablespoon ground ginger

**½ teaspoon ground
cardamom or allspice**

1½ teaspoons baking soda

¼ teaspoon salt

**½ cup chopped kumquat
halves from Kumquat
Conserve (page 14)**

**¾ cup candied or
crystallized ginger**

Cream Cheese Glaze

**1 (4-ounce) package cream
cheese, room temperature**

**3 tablespoons confectioners'
sugar**

2 tablespoons half-and-half

Note: *This batter can also be used to make 12 cupcakes.
Cooking time will be about 30 minutes.*

Preheat oven to 350°F and position a rack in the center of the oven. Grease and flour a 10-inch decorative tube pan, kugelhopf, or Bundt pan.

To make the batter, place butter and brown sugar in the bowl of a stand mixer fitted with the paddle attachment. Beat on medium speed until very light in color, about 4 to 5 minutes. Beat in maple syrup. Add eggs, one at a time, allowing each to blend in fully before adding the next. Scrape down the bowl between additions. Add vanilla and Fuyu Persimmon Purée and blend well. The mixture will look broken, but it will smooth out after the flour is added.

In a separate bowl, whisk together flour, spices, baking soda, and salt. Add this to the batter and beat on low, just until no streaks of flour remain. Fold kumquat pieces and candied ginger into batter.

Pour batter into prepared pan and bake for 45 to 55 minutes, or until a cake tester or toothpick inserted into the center of the cake comes out clean and the top of cake feels firm to the touch. Place pan on rack to cool completely.

To prepare the cream cheese glaze, place all glaze ingredients in the bowl of a stand mixer fitted with the paddle attachment. Beat on medium speed until well combined.

To glaze the cake, unmold it onto a cooling rack set over a sheet pan. Spoon the glaze over the top and let it drip down the sides.

To serve, carefully transfer cake to a plate or cake pedestal.

FUYU PERSIMMON AND BLOOD ORANGE ROULADE WITH CANDIED ORANGE FILLING

Lots of people bake a pumpkin roulade, but why not persimmon? The whipped cream filling is scented with Grand Marnier and a sprinkling of candied orange peel. This is a festive cake that is easy to slice and serve and works well on a buffet.

Makes 1

Preheat oven to 375°F and position a rack in the center of the oven. Line a 12x18x1-inch jellyroll pan with parchment paper.

To prepare the batter, place egg yolks, sugar, and brown sugar in the bowl of a stand mixer fitted with the whisk attachment. Whip on high speed until very thick and light in color, about 3 to 5 minutes. Add Fuyu Persimmon Purée and blend well. In a separate bowl, sift flour and cardamom together, then add to the persimmon mixture and whip until well blended.

Place egg whites in a clean, dry bowl of the stand mixer fitted with a clean whisk attachment. Whip on medium speed until soft peaks form. Immediately fold egg whites into Fuyu persimmon mixture. Pour batter into prepared pan and spread in an even layer. Sprinkle the chopped walnuts over the top.

Bake for 15 minutes, or until a cake tester or toothpick inserted into the center of the cake comes out clean. Remove the cake from the oven and immediately dust it generously with confectioners' sugar. Gently run a knife around the edges of the cake to loosen it from the pan. Place a large sheet of parchment on top of the cake, and holding the two together, carefully flip the cake over. Gently remove the parchment on top and allow cake cool. ››

Batter

6 large eggs, separated and room temperature

⅓ cup granulated sugar

⅓ cup light brown sugar

⅔ cup Fuyu Persimmon Purée (page 13)

¾ cup sifted cake flour

¾ teaspoon ground cardamom

1 cup finely chopped toasted walnuts

⅓ cup confectioners' sugar, for dusting

Syrup

⅓ cup Blood Orange Marmalade (page 15)

2 tablespoons granulated sugar

1 tablespoon Grand Marnier or orange liqueur

1 tablespoon water

Filling

1 cup heavy cream

1 tablespoon granulated sugar

1 teaspoon Grand Marnier or orange liqueur

¼ cup chopped candied orange peel

Finishing Touches

Confectioners' sugar

« To make the syrup, place all syrup ingredients in a small saucepan and heat until sugar dissolves. Do not boil. Keep warm until needed.

To make the filling, place cream, sugar, and liqueur in the bowl of a stand mixer fitted with the whisk attachment, and whip until firm peaks form. Gently fold in the orange peel.

To begin assembling the cake, position the cake so that the long edges are parallel to the edge of your work surface. Spread the warm syrup over the cake; it will be a very thin layer and will soak in immediately.

Spread the filling in an even layer over the surface of the cake, leaving a 1-inch border at the long edge furthest away from you. Rolling away from you, roll the cake snugly, but not so tightly that filling squeezes out. The cake should roll about 1½ times. Finish the roll with the far edge of the cake at the bottom.

Tuck the parchment paper in around the roll, and twist the ends of the paper to help the roll hold its shape. Place on a sheet pan and keep refrigerated until ready to serve, but not more than 2 days.

To serve, unwrap the roulade, remove the parchment paper, and dust with confectioners' sugar. Transfer to a serving platter or simply slice the cake and plate individually. If desired, serve with warm caramel sauce.

PILED HIGH FUYU PERSIMMON PECAN CAKE

*Want an impressive multilayered dessert that doesn't take hours to prepare? This recipe is it —
richly delicious with persimmon spice cake baked on top of a pecan cookie, scrumptious cream
cheese filling and frosting, and finished off with a caramel drizzle. A beautiful tower
crowned with caramel — tell me you're not thinking about baking this!
Serve it on a cake pedestal for a magnificent presentation.*

Makes 1

Pecan Cookie & Spice Cake

**2 cups crushed vanilla
  wafers**

1 cup chopped pecans

**¾ cup unsalted butter,
  room temperature**

1 box spice cake mix

**2 cups Fuyu Persimmon
  Purée (page 13)**

**¼ cup unsalted butter,
  room temperature**

4 eggs

Cream Cheese Filling &
Frosting

⅔ cup unsalted butter

**1 (8-ounce) package cream
  cheese, room temperature**

**3 cups sifted confectioners'
  sugar**

**1 teaspoon ginger extract or
  ½ teaspoon ground ginger**

Caramel

¼ cup water

1 cup granulated sugar

**1¾ cups heavy cream,
  warmed**

Note: *Feel free to substitute high-quality, store-bought caramel
sauce.*

Preheat oven to 350°F and position a rack in the center of
the oven. Grease and flour three round 8- or 9-inch cake pans.

To make the pecan cookie and spice cake layer, combine the
first three ingredients in a bowl and press into the prepared pans.
Next, place cake mix, Fuyu Persimmon Purée, butter, and eggs
in the bowl of a stand mixer fitted with the paddle attachment.
Beat until smooth. Divide and spread the persimmon cake batter evenly over the pecan cookie in each pan. Bake for about 25
minutes, or until a cake tester or toothpick inserted in the center
comes out clean. Cool in pans and then turn out onto racks.

To make the cream cheese filling and frosting, place butter,
cream cheese, sugar, and ginger in the bowl of a stand mixer
fitted with the paddle attachment. Beat until light and creamy.

To make the caramel, place water and sugar in a medium
saucepan and cook over medium-low heat. Stir constantly until
the sugar dissolves and liquid is clear. Raise heat to high and
cook until golden brown. Immediately remove pan from heat
and add warmed cream. Be careful! The mixture will bubble
furiously! If there are any hardened bits of caramel, set the pan
over low heat and stir to melt. Cool to room temperature.

To assemble, place one pecan cookie and spice cake on a
plate or cake pedestal. Spread with about one-third of the
cream cheese mixture. Top with another pecan cookie and spice
cake and more cream cheese. Place the third pecan cookie and
spice cake on top and frost with remaining cream cheese. Pour
caramel sauce over the top and let it drip down the sides. Keep
refrigerated, but bring to room temperature before serving.

CARAMEL-GLAZED FUYU PERSIMMON SPICE CAKE

Persimmons, pecans, and autumn spices — another winning combination. This cake stays very moist because of the Fuyu Persimmon Purée, making it a delicious dessert or snack over several days...if it lasts that long. It's perfect with tea on a chilly fall afternoon.

Makes 1

To make the glaze, place water and honey in a saucepan over low heat. Add sugar and cook, stirring gently, until sugar dissolves and liquid is clear. Raise heat to high and cook until golden brown. Immediately remove pan from heat and add cream. Be careful! The mixture will bubble furiously! If there are any hardened bits of caramel, set the pan over low heat and stir to melt. Pour into a heatproof bowl and cool to room temperature. Then refrigerate to thicken. This can be made and refrigerated up to 5 days in advance.

Preheat oven to 350°F and position a rack in the center of the oven. Grease and flour a 10-inch Bundt pan.

To make the batter, place butter and sugars in the bowl of a stand mixer fitted with the paddle attachment. Beat on medium speed until very light in color, about 4 to 5 minutes. Add eggs, one at a time, allowing each to blend in fully before adding the next. Scrape down the bowl between additions. Beat in Fuyu Persimmon Purée and vanilla until well combined. Sift together all dry ingredients and add to wet mixture in batches alternating with buttermilk. Mix well after each addition. Stir in chopped persimmons and pecans.

To bake the cake, pour batter into prepared pan and bake for 40 to 45 minutes, or until a cake tester or toothpick inserted in the center of the cake comes out clean and the cake is firm to the touch. Place pan on a rack to cool completely.

To glaze the cake, transfer it to a plate or cake pedestal and bring the caramel glaze to room temperature. Spoon caramel sauce over the top of the cake, letting it drip down the sides.

Serve at room temperature.

Glaze

- ¼ cup water
- 1 tablespoon honey
- 1 cup granulated sugar
- ¾ cup heavy cream, warmed

Batter

- ½ cup (1 stick) unsalted butter, room temperature
- 1 cup granulated sugar
- ⅓ cup light brown sugar
- 2 large eggs, room temperature
- 1 cup Fuyu Persimmon Purée (page 13)
- 1 teaspoon pure vanilla extract
- 2 cups sifted cake flour
- ¼ teaspoon baking soda
- 1 teaspoon baking powder
- ½ teaspoon ground ginger
- ½ teaspoon freshly ground nutmeg
- Pinch salt
- ½ cup buttermilk, room temperature
- ½ cup chopped Dried Fuyu Persimmon Slices (page 13)
- ¾ cup toasted and chopped pecans

TRIPLE LAYER FUYU PERSIMMON PIE

By now you've deduced that I love multilayered desserts. Here's another. This pie features Fuyu persimmon custard, persimmon mousse, and fresh whipped cream. When you make this, I suggest you skip dinner and go straight for dessert!

Makes 1

Crust

1 pre-baked homemade graham cracker or gingersnap crust (page 57)

Custard

1 large egg plus 1 yolk

3 tablespoons firmly packed light brown sugar

½ cup Fuyu Persimmon Purée (page 13)

⅓ cup heavy cream

¼ teaspoon ground cardamom

⅛ teaspoon ground ginger

⅛ teaspoon pure almond extract

Pecan Praline

¾ cup toasted pecan pieces

¼ cup water

½ cup granulated sugar

Mousse

1 tablespoon dark rum

1 tablespoon water

2¼ teaspoons powdered unflavored gelatin

½ cup heavy cream

2 eggs

3 tablespoons firmly packed light brown sugar

¼ teaspoon ground cinnamon

⅛ teaspoon ground ginger

⅛ teaspoon ground allspice

½ cup Fuyu Persimmon Purée (page 13)

¼ cup ground pecan praline ››

Preheat oven to 325°F and position a rack in the center of the oven. Lightly grease a sheet pan and set aside.

Prepare homemade crust.

To make the custard, mix all custard ingredients until well combined. Pour into the pre-baked pie shell. Bake for 12 to 15 minutes, or just until set in the center. Place pie on a rack to cool completely. Refrigerate until needed.

To make the pecan praline, place toasted nuts very close together in a single layer in the center of the prepared sheet pan. In a medium saucepan, heat water and sugar until sugar dissolves and liquid is clear. Raise the heat to high and boil rapidly. Swirl the pan occasionally, but do not stir, so the sugar cooks evenly and turns a golden brown. Immediately pour caramel over nuts. Set aside to cool completely. Break into pieces and transfer to a food processor, then pulse until finely ground. Store in an airtight container at room temperature. This can be done several days in advance.

To prepare the gelatin for the mousse, combine rum and water in a small bowl. Sprinkle gelatin over the liquid and stir gently to make sure all the granules are moistened; let sit for 5 minutes. Place the small bowl in a larger bowl of hot, but not boiling, water, and stir mixture until the liquid warms and the gelatin completely dissolves. Set aside.

To make the whipped cream for the mousse, pour the heavy cream into the bowl of a stand mixer fitted with the whisk attachment and whip to soft peaks. Transfer the whipped cream to a small bowl and refrigerate until needed. Do not wash the mixer bowl or whisk.

Place eggs and brown sugar in the top of a double boiler and whisk constantly, until mixture begins to lighten and look like soft whipped cream. Remove when the temperature reaches 160°F on an instant-read thermometer. Pour into the used bowl of the stand mixer fitted with the used whisk attachment and whip on high speed until very light in color and cool to the touch. Whip in the spices, then the Fuyu Persimmon Purée, ››

Topping

1¼ cups heavy cream

1 tablespoon granulated sugar

1 teaspoon pure vanilla extract

‹‹ and the gelatin. Blend well between additions. Fold in the reserved whipped cream until no streaks remain, and the ground pecan praline. Pour immediately onto the custard layer of the baked pie until it comes up to the top of the crust. Refrigerate until set, at least 2 hours.

To make the topping, place heavy cream, sugar, and vanilla into a clean, dry bowl of the stand mixer fitted with a clean whisk attachment, and whip to firm peaks. Transfer to a pastry bag fitted and pipe topping to completely cover the mousse layer. Keep refrigerated until ready to serve.

CHOCOLATE COOKIE PIE CRUST

Makes 1 (9-inch) pie crust

30 chocolate cookie wafers

1 teaspoon vanilla extract

½ teaspoon salt

¼ cup unsalted butter, melted

Preheat oven to 350°F and position a rack in center of the oven.

Place all ingredients in the bowl of the food processor and pulse until the ingredients are well blended and start to form a ball. Firmly press the crumb mixture into the bottom and up the sides of a 9-inch pie dish. Bake until the crust is set, about 10 to 12 minutes. Let cool completely on a wire rack.

GRAHAM CRACKER PIE CRUST

Makes 1 (9-inch) pie crust

¾ cup graham cracker crumbs

2½ ounces almond paste

¼ cup granulated sugar

¼ teaspoon salt

⅓ cup unsalted butter, melted

Preheat oven to 350°F and position a rack in center of the oven.

Combine all ingredients in a medium bowl and mix until well blended. Firmly press the crumb mixture into the bottom and up the sides of a 9-inch pie dish. Bake until the crust is set, about 10 to 12 minutes. Let cool completely on a wire rack.

JEWELS FROM

57

MY GROVE

GINGERSNAP PIE CRUST

Makes 1 (9-inch) pie crust

1½ cups gingersnap crumbs

3 tablespoons granulated sugar

½ teaspoon salt

1 teaspoon crystallized ginger, minced

¼ cup unsalted butter, melted

Preheat oven to 350°F and position a rack in center of the oven.

Combine all ingredients in a medium bowl. Firmly press the crumb mixture into the bottom and up the sides of a 9-inch pie dish. Bake until the crust is set, about 10 minutes. Let cool completely on a wire rack.

ALL SEASON FUYU PERSIMMON, BLOOD ORANGE, AND PECAN PIE

Just because Fuyu persimmons are harvested in the fall doesn't mean you can't bake with them year-round. Persimmon purée freezes beautifully and can last in the freezer for 12 months. So if you're hankering for a persimmon pie in April, you can make it! This one features a full-bodied persimmon filling finished with a caramelized pecan topping.

Makes 1

Crust

1 pre-baked homemade chocolate or your choice crust (page 57)

Filling

1½ cups Fuyu Persimmon Purée (page 13)

½ cup granulated sugar

½ teaspoon salt

½ teaspoon ground ginger

3 eggs

¼ cup blood orange juice

2 tablespoons bourbon

¾ cup half-and-half

Topping

⅔ cup light brown sugar

3 tablespoons unsalted butter, melted

1 tablespoon heavy cream

½ teaspoon salt

½ cup chopped pecans

Finishing Touch

Pecan halves

Preheat oven to 375°F and position a rack in the center of the oven.

To make the filling, place all filling ingredients in the bowl of a stand mixer fitted with the paddle attachment, and beat until well combined. Pour into pie crust. Bake for 15 minutes. Lower heat to 350°F and bake 30 minutes more, or until filling is set. Place pie on a rack to cool until lukewarm. Change oven setting to broil.

To make the topping, mix all topping ingredients except pecan halves in a small bowl. Pour over pie and decorate with pecan halves. With the rack still in the center of the oven, return the pie to the oven just until the topping is bubbly. Watch carefully to avoid burning the pie!

Fuyu Persimmon Sour Cream Torte

Seven cookie-like layers slathered with an unbelievably luscious Fuyu persimmon filling.

Makes 1

Preheat oven to 350°F and position a rack in the center of the oven.

To make the cookie dough, place flour and sugar in a bowl and, using a pastry blender or two knives, work butter into flour mixture until it becomes soft and crumbly. Stir in egg. With your hands, mix until the dough sticks together, then divide into seven equal parts. Between two pieces of parchment, roll each piece into a very thin 7-inch circle. Remove top piece of parchment. You can leave the circle as is or use a 7-inch round plate as a guide to trim the edges. Lifting the bottom sheet of parchment, place the cookie and parchment on a sheet pan.

Bake each circle for 10 to 12 minutes, or until the edges begin to brown lightly. Cool the cookie on the sheet pan before carefully transferring it on the parchment to the work surface.

Repeat rolling out remaining dough between parchment and baking circles, allowing the pan to cool between bakings.

To make the filling, mix all filling ingredients.

To assemble the torte, carefully spread the first six cookie layers with filling and stack on a plate or cake pedestal. Place last cookie layer and sift confectioners' sugar over the top. Refrigerate for 5 hours or best overnight before serving.

Cookie Dough

3 cups sifted unbleached all-purpose flour

¾ cup granulated sugar

1 cup (2 sticks) unsalted butter

1 egg

Filling

2 cups finely chopped walnuts

2 cups sour cream

1½ cups confectioners' sugar

1 teaspoon pure vanilla extract

⅔ cup Fuyu Persimmon Purée (page 13)

Finishing Touch

Confectioners' sugar

ABOUT TORTES

Originally from Central Europe, tortes are multilayered cakes with buttercream, mousse, jam, or other delicious ingredients. Probably the most famous torte is the Austrian *Sachertorte*, a rich chocolate sponge cake glazed with apricot jam and coated with bittersweet chocolate ganache. The *Linzertorte*, with its nutty crust, fruity filling, and lattice top, hails from Austria, and the luscious Black Forest Cake, as we call it, is a torte layered with chocolate cake, whipped cream, and sweetened sour cherries. It is sometimes drenched in Kirsch, a cherry liqueur. In German, it is called a Black Forest cherry torte or *Schwarzwälder Kirschtorte*. Hungary is famous for its *Dobos* torte or *Dobosh*, named after József C. Dobos, the pastry chef who first created it and chocolate buttercream. Prior to that, most cake fillings were cooked pastry cream or whipped cream. The *Dobos* torte is made of five or more thin layers of sponge cake with chocolate buttercream and caramel topping.

Fuyu Persimmon Tarte Tatin

You've usually seen Tarte Tatin done with apples or pears, but my version uses fresh Fuyu persimmons. I've chosen to make these as individual tarts because a ripe Fuyu persimmon fits perfectly into an individual ramekin and makes the dessert a bit more fun.

Makes 6 (4-inch) tarts

Persimmons

6 ripe, but not too firm, Fuyu persimmons (about 3½ ounces each), peeled with calyx sliced off the top

2 tablespoons brandy, Amaretto, or your favorite liqueur

Dough

1 cup unbleached all-purpose flour

¼ teaspoon salt

6 tablespoons cold unsalted butter, cut into ½-inch pieces

2 ounces almond paste, cut into ½-inch pieces

¼ cup cold water

Caramel

4 tablespoons unsalted butter

½ cup granulated sugar

To prepare the Fuyu persimmons, place the peeled persimmons and liqueur in a zip-top plastic bag, seal, and allow to marinate for 30 minutes at room temperature.

To make the dough, place flour and salt in the bowl of a food processor and run for 10 seconds to blend well. Add butter and process in pulses until butter is the size of large peas. Add almond paste and continue to pulse until paste and butter are in pieces no larger than small peas. (Some will be much smaller, and this is fine). Add cold water and pulse until the mixture begins to look crumbly. Do not let it form a ball. Remove from the machine and knead 2 or 3 times, just to bring the dough together. If the dough seems very soft or sticky, chill for 1 hour. When ready, dust work surface with flour and roll out dough into a ¼-inch-thick circle. Using a 3½-inch round biscuit cutter or drinking glass, cut out 6 rounds. Brush any excess flour from the rounds, place on a sheet pan lined with parchment, and refrigerate for at least 2 hours.

Coat 6 (4-inch) round ramekins with nonstick spray and set aside.

To make the caramel, place the butter and sugar in a small saucepan over medium heat. Cook, stirring often, until the mixture turns a golden brown color. You will need to stir »

« continuously toward the end. Immediately remove the pan from the heat and divide the caramel among the ramekins or custard cups. Let the caramel cool and harden. Cover with plastic wrap and leave at room temperature. This step can be done one day in advance.

Preheat oven to 375°F and position a rack in the center of the oven. Place a Fuyu persimmon, cut side down, in each caramel-lined ramekin. Top each with a circle of dough, tucking the edges down around fruit. Place the ramekins on a sheet pan and bake for 40 to 45 minutes, or until the fruit is tender and the crust is cooked through and browned. Remove the pan from the oven and allow tarts to cool for 10 minutes. Invert onto plates and serve.

ABOUT THE TARTE TATIN

Part of the magic of a Tarte Tatin, or upside down tart, is that the fruit is pre-cooked in sugar and butter so it caramelizes, and the crust is placed on top of the fruit before baking. Originally this dessert was made with only certain apple varieties that would soften and caramelize without entirely losing their shape when baked.

There are several theories about the origin of the Tarte Tatin, and many scholars have researched its history. One story goes that in the 1880s, the Tarte Tatin was created by accident at the Hotel Tatin, located south of Paris, One of two sisters who owned the hotel, Stephanie Tatin, was making an apple pie, but she overcooked the apples, sugar, and butter on the stovetop. Her quick fix? She covered it with a sheet of pastry and put the entire pan in the oven.

Another story suggests that Stephanie dropped an apple tart as she rushed through the kitchen, quickly picked it up, rearranged it in the pan, and popped it back in the oven. After baking it, she flipped it out onto a plate, and the famous Tarte Tatin was born. The recipe was never published, and Stephanie never labeled it "Tarte Tatin." It was named by Maurice Edmond Sailland, dubbed the Prince of Gastronomy and better known by his pen name, Curnonsky. He was the most celebrated culinary writer in France, in the twentieth century. The Tarte Tatin finally gained fame at Maxim's in Paris.

The most astounding part of the Tarte Tatin is that historians, chefs, and food writers have studied and written about this humble dessert for more than 100 years. Entire books and websites have been written about this French dessert, pondering whether it was created by an accident in the kitchen or by a truly original baker.

Fuyu Persimmon Biscotti with Ginger and Cardamom

Enjoy biscotti with cappuccino, your favorite tea, or Vin Santo (Italian dessert wine). But don't order a biscotti when you're in Italy unless you want any flavor of twice-baked cookie. For a true almond biscotti, Italians ask for cantucci.

Makes 60 to 70

¾ cup (1½ sticks) unsalted butter, room temperature

1½ cups firmly packed light brown sugar

3 large eggs

2 teaspoons pure vanilla extract

¾ cup Fuyu Persimmon Purée (page 13)

3 cups unbleached all-purpose flour

2 teaspoons ground cardamom

1 teaspoon baking powder

¼ teaspoon salt

½ cup crystallized or candied ginger

1 cup chopped toasted walnuts

Preheat oven to 350°F and position a rack in the center of the oven. Stack two sheet pans on top of each other and line the top pan with parchment paper.

Place butter and sugar in the bowl of a stand mixer fitted with the paddle attachment and beat on medium speed until light in color, about 4 to 5 minutes. Add eggs, one at a time, allowing each to blend in before adding the next. Scrape down the bowl between additions. Add vanilla and Fuyu Persimmon Purée, and blend thoroughly. In a separate bowl, whisk flour, cardamom, baking powder, and salt, and add to the batter. Beat just until combined. Fold in ginger and walnuts. Dough will be wet and sticky.

Divide dough in half and form two logs the length of the top parchment-lined sheet pan. Bake for 35 to 40 minutes, or until firm and golden brown. Remove the second sheet pan, and place the pan with the biscotti on a rack to cool. When cool, gently cut each log into ½-inch-thick diagonal slices.

Lower oven to 300°F. Line sheet pans with parchment paper.

Divide the cookies between prepared sheet pans. Toast for 15 to 20 minutes on each side. When you flip the cookies, rotate the pans in the oven for the final toasting. Cool on racks. If they are still a bit soft, return to the oven and toast further. Will keep for about 2 weeks stored in an airtight container.

ABOUT BISCOTTI

Biscotti date back to Roman times. These dry, biscuit-like cookies were a staple for the Roman Legions because of their durability and resistance to spoiling. The Italian word *biscotto* is from the Latin *bis*, meaning twice, and *coctum*, or baked. After the fall of the Roman Empire, the region was plundered by numerous invaders, and there was little in the way of culinary development. But with the Renaissance, food and wine flowered along with the arts, and the biscotti reemerged in Tuscany, popularized by a Tuscan baker who served them with sweet wine for dipping. Because almonds were widely grown in the region, Tuscan biscotti were flavored with almonds. As the cookie's popularity spread, each region added its own unique ingredients.

FUYU PERSIMMON CREAM CHEESE TEA CAKE

Depending on where you live, the words "tea cake" conjure up different kinds of cakes, breads, cookies, or even biscuits. In the southeastern part of the United States, a tea cake often refers to a large, dense round cookie. Elsewhere in the U.S., it is a single-layer unfrosted cake sometimes made with fruits or nuts. In England, a tea cake is usually a lightly sweetened yeast bun or roll that is sliced, toasted, and served with tea. My version is a lightly spiced, moist cake with a cream cheese filling, baked in a loaf pan.

Makes 1

Preheat oven to 350°F and position a rack in the center of the oven. Lightly grease and flour or coat a 9x5-inch loaf pan with nonstick spray.

To make the filling, place cream cheese and sugar in the bowl of a stand mixer fitted with the paddle attachment. Beat on medium speed until smooth and creamy. Add whole egg first, allowing it to blend in fully before adding the yolk. Scrape down the bowl between additions. Beat in vanilla. Add flour and blend well. Set aside.

To make the batter, place eggs and sugar in a large bowl and whisk well. Stir in Fuyu Persimmon Purée. Whisk in melted butter until well combined. In a separate bowl, gently whisk flour, baking soda, cardamom, ginger, salt, and cloves. Add this to the batter and mix until no streaks of flour remain. Pour half of the batter into the prepared pan. Top with all but 1 tablespoon of the filling. Spoon remaining batter over the filling. You will likely see a bit of filling around the edges. Drizzle the remaining filling over the top.

Bake for 1 hour, or until a cake tester or toothpick inserted into the center comes out with just a few moist crumbs and the top feels firm to the touch. The visible filling will have turned a golden brown. Don't over-bake or the cake will become dry. Place pan on a rack to cool completely.

Serve cold or at room temperature. Wrap tightly or transfer to an airtight container and refrigerate. This cake also freezes well and will last up to 2 months if carefully wrapped.

Filling

6 ounces cream cheese, room temperature

⅓ cup granulated sugar

1 large egg plus 1 egg yolk

½ teaspoon pure vanilla extract

1½ tablespoons unbleached all-purpose flour

Batter

2 large eggs

1½ cups granulated sugar

1⅓ cups Fuyu Persimmon Purée (page 14)

½ cup (1 stick) unsalted butter, melted

1⅔ cups unbleached all-purpose flour

½ teaspoon baking soda

1 teaspoon ground cardamom

½ teaspoon ground ginger

¼ teaspoon salt

Pinch ground cloves

Lemon-Glazed Fuyu Persimmon Muffins

When we have overnight company and I want to serve something special in the morning, I have two go-to breakfast recipes, and this is one of them. The other is Kumquat Scones with Blood Orange Zest and Candied Ginger on page 148. These muffins are incredibly moist with a delicate flavor, and they keep well for several days.

Makes 12

Batter

½ cup granulated sugar

¼ cup honey

½ cup (1 stick) unsalted butter, room temperature

1 egg

1 cup Fuyu Persimmon Purée (page 13)

3 tablespoons fresh lemon juice

2 cups unbleached all-purpose flour

1 teaspoon baking powder

½ teaspoon baking soda

½ teaspoon salt

½ cup chopped walnuts

Glaze

¾ cup sifted confectioners' sugar

1 tablespoon fresh lemon juice

½ teaspoon pure vanilla extract

Preheat oven to 350°F and position a rack in the center of the oven. Lightly grease a 12-cup muffin pan or use paper liners.

To make the batter, place sugar, honey, and butter in the bowl of a stand mixer fitted with the paddle attachment and beat at medium-high speed until light and fluffy. Add egg, Fuyu Persimmon Purée, and lemon juice and blend thoroughly. In a separate bowl, whisk flour, baking powder, baking soda, and salt. Add this mixture to the batter and beat just until combined. Stir in chopped walnuts. Fill muffin cups three-quarters full. Bake 25 to 30 minutes, or until cake tester or toothpick inserted into the center comes out clean. Place on a rack to cool for 5 minutes.

To make the glaze, place all glaze ingredients in a small bowl and whisk until smooth.

Spread or drizzle glaze over warm muffins. I love the muffins best when warm, but they are delicious at room temperature, too. Store in an airtight container.

Fuyu Persimmon Panna Cotta

Italy is the world's fifth-largest persimmon producer and is also the home of panna cotta, the luscious dessert made from cream, milk, sugar, and gelatin. The Italians sure have good taste! Combine the sweet creamy texture of panna cotta with the ripe persimmon and you'll understand why the Greeks called the persimmon "the fruit of the gods."

Serves 6 to 8

Lightly grease or coat 6 (8-ounce) or 8 (6-ounce) custard cups or ramekins with nonstick spray.

To make the caramel, place water and sugar in a medium saucepan and heat slowly until sugar dissolves and liquid is clear. Turn the heat to high and boil rapidly. Swirl the pan occasionally, but do not stir, so sugar cooks evenly, until it turns golden brown. Remove the pan from the heat and, working quickly, pour caramel in each cup or mold, then carefully swirl each cup to distribute the caramel evenly around the sides to about ¼ inch from the lip. Pour any excess back into the saucepan.

To prepare the gelatin, place milk in a small bowl. Sprinkle gelatin over the liquid, and stir to make sure all the granules are moistened. Set aside for at least 5 minutes.

To make the panna cotta, place cream, milk, brown sugar, cardamom seeds, and ginger in a medium saucepan. Heat slowly just to the scalding point. Remove from the heat, cover with a lid, and allow mixture to steep for 15 minutes, then add gelatin mixture, gently stirring until granules completely dissolve. Whisk in Fuyu Persimmon Purée, blending well. Discard cardamom and ginger. Divide mixture among the prepared cups or molds. Cover and refrigerate to set, at least 3 to 4 hours.

To serve, dip each mold into hot water for a just few seconds to loosen the panna cotta and invert onto plates.

Note: *To remove any hardened caramel from the saucepan, fill it with water and bring to a boil for about 10 minutes. The caramel will just melt away into the hot water. Pour boiling water into the ramekins to clean them as well.*

Caramel
¼ cup water

1 cup granulated sugar

Gelatin
½ cup whole milk

2 teaspoons powdered unflavored gelatin

Panna Cotta
1 cup heavy cream

½ cup whole milk

¼ cup firmly packed light brown sugar

½ teaspoon cardamom seeds

5 slices fresh ginger, each about the size of a nickel and ⅓-inch thick

1 cup Fuyu Persimmon Purée (page 13)

Fuyu Persimmon Pudding Cake

Here's another easy dessert that's delicious and quick to prepare. Cooked puddings are more intensely flavorful served warm, right from the oven. If you keep Fuyu Persimmon Purée in your freezer, you can whip this up in minutes.

Makes 1 (8-inch) or 8 (4-inch) puddings

Batter

2 cups Fuyu Persimmon Purée (page 13)

3 eggs

1¼ cups granulated sugar

1½ cups unbleached all-purpose flour

1 teaspoon baking powder

1 teaspoon baking soda

½ teaspoon salt

½ cup (1 stick) unsalted butter, melted

2½ cups whole milk

1 teaspoon ground ginger

½ to 2 teaspoons freshly grated nutmeg, depending upon desired spiciness or coloring

Finishing Touches

Whipped cream, if desired

Chopped pecans, if desired

Preheat oven to 325°F and position a rack in the center of the oven. Lightly coat 1 (8-inch) mold or 8 individual molds with nonstick spray.

To make the batter, thoroughly combine all batter ingredients in a bowl. Pour into prepared molds and bake until firm, about 1 hour. Place on racks to cool.

To serve, invert mold or molds and garnish with homemade whipped cream and chopped pecans, if desired.

Fuyu Persimmon Caramel Ice Cream

If I could eat only one flavor of ice cream for the rest of my life, this would be the one. Enough said — it really is that good! I have yet to serve this ice cream when everyone hasn't raved about the flavor and creaminess.

Makes about 1 quart

Note: *Ice cream base needs 24 hours or overnight to chill and "ripen" before freezing in an ice cream machine.*

To begin the ice cream base, heat cream, milk, and sugar to scalding in a large saucepan. Turn off heat and leave the saucepan on the stove to stay warm.

To make the caramel, slowly heat water and sugar in a medium saucepan until sugar dissolves and liquid is clear. Turn the heat to high and boil rapidly. Swirl the pan occasionally, but do not stir, so the sugar cooks evenly, until it turns golden brown. Remove the pan from the heat and immediately slowly pour it into the warm cream mixture, whisking constantly. Be careful! The mixture will bubble furiously in the pan. If there are any hardened bits of caramel, set the pan over low heat and stir to melt. Set caramel cream aside and let cool for 30 minutes or place in an ice bath until lukewarm.

To finish the ice cream base, place egg yolks in a small bowl and whisk lightly, just to blend. Pour about 1 cup of warm caramel cream into the yolks, whisking constantly. Pour the yolk mixture back into the saucepan and cook over low heat, stirring constantly, until the custard thickens and coats the back of a spoon and registers 180°F on an instant-read thermometer. Pour through a fine-mesh strainer into a clean bowl and whisk in the Fuyu Persimmon Purée, vanilla and almond extracts, and spices. Cool completely in the refrigerator, allowing the ice cream to "ripen" for 24 hours in the refrigerator before freezing.

Freeze in an ice cream machine according to manufacturer's instructions. Ice cream will stay fresh in the freezer for about 1 month if properly sealed.

Ice Cream, Step 1
1½ cups heavy cream
½ cup whole milk
¼ cup granulated sugar

Caramel
¼ cup water
½ cup plus 2 tablespoons granulated sugar

Ice Cream, Step 2
5 large egg yolks
1 cup Fuyu Persimmon Purée (page 13)
2 teaspoons pure vanilla extract
½ teaspoon pure almond extract
¼ teaspoon ground ginger
¼ teaspoon ground cardamom

KUMQUATS

Consider the Kumquat

An excerpt from "Consider the Kumquat" by Justine Sterling,
originally published in *Saveur* magazine

"As a young girl growing up on a California vineyard,
I passed the long summers outdoors, and when I wasn't catching lizards or
squeezing grapes into fizzy water in order to make 'wine spritzers,' I was foraging.
I picked miner's lettuce from the wet grass, wine grapes from their vines, thick-skinned
grapefruit that had no business growing that far north, and even the occasional ant,
just to remind myself what they tasted like. But my favorite treats were the kumquats
that grew in two barrels outside my father's office. The trees the fruits adorned like early
Christmas ornaments stood four feet tall and were laden with glossy, dark green leaves
and white, star-like blossoms. I'd seek shade from the midday sun behind their branches,
pluck handfuls of the oblong orange fruit, and gobble them up in two bites. Each one
exploded in my mouth with tart, pleasing bitterness, and I'd eat until the acid burned
my lips, leaving just enough fruit on each tree to disguise my gluttony.

As far as I can remember, though, I was the only one in my family putting the petite
fruit to use. Indeed, even now, in an era when many cooks don't bat an eyelash at
sunchokes, sea urchin, or pigs' trotters, the kumquat retains an air of mystery. Perhaps
that's because the kumquat is at once like an orange and the opposite of one, with a skin
that is sweet and a fruit that is sour (which explains why most recipes call for using both
the rind and the fruit together). Peeling small orange citrus fruits seems to be a habit
that's hard for Americans to break, but try to peel a kumquat and you'll end up with
nothing but sticky hands and a small, pulpy mass to show for your efforts.

With far-flung fruits like the mangosteen and the durian showing up on local
supermarket shelves, isn't it about time we embraced our own exotics? Give the kumquat
a chance. It may seem backward at first — sweet rind, bitter fruit — but this tiny
gem will surprise and delight you. Just heed these words of caution
from my 7-year-old self: they're acidic and addictive."

Kumquats: Golden Sweet Tarts

YES, YOU EAT THE SKIN, TOO! I CAN'T TELL YOU how many times I've answered that question about kumquats in the last 30 years. When it comes to citrus, we eat the juicy fruit inside and throw out the peel, but kumquats are just the opposite — their flesh is tart, the rind sweet, and they are delicious eaten whole.

Most people look at a kumquat and think, "What an adorable little baby orange," but kumquats are anything but that. If you haven't had the pleasure of eating a fresh kumquat, you must! Looking at this tiny gem-like fruit, you would expect a delicate orange flavor. Its diminutive size provides no clue to its taste. Kumquats pack a real pow. When you first bite into one, you get a sweet burst of flavor from the oils in the skin, and then, bam! The juicy wet pulp throws you a left jab with its puckering tartness.

The kumquat, which hails from Southeast China, appears in Chinese texts as early as the twelfth century and gets its name from the Cantonese *kam kwat*, meaning "golden orange." It grows abundantly in the hills of Hunan, China, where the climate is perfect for this little gem and tea plants, but too cold for other citrus fruits. Although often considered a type of citrus, kumquats actually have their own genus, *Fortunella*, named in honor of Robert Fortune, the horticulturist who introduced kumquats to Europe in 1846 and claimed they were different than other citrus fruits.

There are six varieties of kumquats grown throughout the world, and of these, the Nagami is the most common and our choice for Beck Grove. Kumquats grow on evergreen

trees with beautiful bright green leaves and small white star-like flowers that perfume the air when blooming. The fruit, which can stay on the branches for months without rotting, is a tiny oval, about the size of a large Spanish olive. Its skin is smooth and shiny and ranges in color from yellow-orange to deep warm orange. The kumquat can be stored at room temperature for a couple days and in the refrigerator for two weeks.

These slow-growing trees require a hot summer, are frost-hardy, and can withstand much colder weather than other citrus trees. Kumquats grow better and produce larger and sweeter fruits in warmer regions, so the majority of the fruit is raised in California, Florida, and Texas. At Beck Grove, where our summer ranges from 80°F to 100°F and winter nights rarely get below 40°F, we have great success with the Nagami. Besides being commercially raised, kumquat trees do well in pots as ornamentals and even as bonsais, and with their dark, shiny leaves in contrast to their bright orange fruits, they are often used for decorations.

I love this versatile and delightful fruit, and my goal is to raise its profile and move it from under the radar to a more heroic

status. Like Dade County, Florida, which honors the "golden orange" with an annual festival, I, too, celebrate the kumquat with more than 30 delicious recipes for both sweet and savory dishes. Kumquats can be used much as oranges are in cooking, and they are gradually showing up in more culinary applications — paired with meat, fish, and poultry; in chutneys, marmalades, and jams; sliced and tossed into salads for a refreshing tang; and baked into a vast variety of desserts.

Kumquats are even finding their way into cocktails. They are replacing olives in martinis, showing up in mojitos, and imparting their sweet oil to vodka infusions. Kumquat liqueurs are becoming more popular, too, with their unique, fresh flavor. Try the Koum Kouat of Corfu, Greece. It is a pleasant liqueur made from kumquat fruits, with an aroma and taste that resemble oranges and strawberries, and is exclusively produced on the island of Corfu, where kumquat trees grow prolifically.

The kumquat's roots go deep in Chinese culture. While it has become a symbol of prosperity over the centuries, it also emerged at the center of some special family traditions, writes anthropologist Sidney Cheung. These most likely arose out of rural communities making the most of what limited supplies they had. Cheung believed that these families soon "realized that some items became more valuable or better the longer they kept them." Preserved foods are a great example. Amy Ma, a chef and food writer, notes that many foods, such as preserved fruits, teas, and sauces, are passed down through generations, and she tells this charming story:

"The culinary legacy in Kenneth Tong's family — ham gum guat, Cantonese for 'preserved salted kumquats' — isn't worth much on the street, but it has a priceless personal value.

For as long as Mr. Tong can remember, after every Lunar New Year, his family has assembled and together picked the fruit off kumquat trees, purchased as auspicious decoration during the season because the yellow citrus resembles a golden nugget. The kumquats are cured in a glass jar with salt. In time — about three years, according to Mr. Tong — the once-bright fruit turns dark and floats in an amber-tinged solution.

Each year, new jars are made and left to cure. The older, the better. When mixed with honey and hot water, says 35-year-old Mr. Tong, the pickled fruit tastes lively and refreshing.

'These kumquats are often given to daughters during weddings as a blessing and part of their dowry, since it is believed that those greater than 20 years old develop medicinal properties that can fix a seasonal cough,' says Mr. Tong, a Hong Kong native and self-described foodie.

At the age of 5, he accidentally broke one of his grandmother's 25-year-old jars of preserved kumquats. Today his mother's batch, just 15 years old, is underdeveloped in comparison. 'I don't know if the magic really works,' says Mr. Tong. 'But I can feel the love in it.'"

Given the love we Americans have for trying new tastes from around the world, it's high time we enrich our culinary history with the tiny but mighty kumquat. Embrace its inside-out deliciousness — the sweet skin, the tart and sour flesh — and bring this orange gem into your culinary repertoire.

SCALLOP AND FENNEL SALAD WITH KUMQUAT AND BLOOD ORANGE VINAIGRETTE

This light and easy entrée salad combines the sweet tartness of kumquats and the licorice of fennel, a perfect match for seafood. You might want to double the vinaigrette because it's great on all kinds of salads. You can substitute shrimp or your favorite fish for the scallops.

Serves 4

Vinaigrette

¼ cup liquid from Kumquat Conserve (page 14)

¼ cup rice vinegar

¼ teaspoon salt

1 small shallot, diced

¼ cup blood orange juice

¾ cup olive or grapeseed oil

Salt and freshly ground black pepper, to taste

Salad

4 fennel bulbs, sliced paper-thin

1 red bell pepper, diced

½ cup kumquat halves from Kumquat Conserve (page 14)

6 to 8 cups baby greens

Scallops

Peanut oil, for frying

12 to 16 large sea scallops

Salt and freshly ground black pepper, to taste

Finishing Touch

Leafy fennel fronds

To make the vinaigrette, combine the Kumquat Conserve liquid, vinegar, salt, shallot, blood orange juice and whisk well. Drizzle oil in and whisk until blended. Adjust seasoning. Refrigerate.

To prepare the salad, combine fennel slices, red pepper, and kumquat halves in a bowl. Gently toss with greens. Refrigerate until needed.

To cook the scallops, heat 2 tablespoons of oil in a skillet over medium-high heat. Season scallops with salt and pepper and place half of them in the hot pan, searing until brown, and turning only once to sear the other side. Remove from pan and drain on paper towels. Add more oil to pan if needed, and finish cooking the remaining scallops.

Plate the prepared greens, top with 3 or 4 scallops and fennel fronds, drizzle with kumquat vinaigrette, and serve.

ABOUT FENNEL

Fennel grows prolifically throughout most of the United States, southern Canada, Australia, Asia, and the Middle East. It is thought to have originated in the dry, hot Mediterranean climate because the seeds, bulb, and leaves are featured in many Mediterranean cuisines. The Greek name for fennel is *marathos*, and Marathon, the Greek city and site of many sporting events, literally means "a plain with fennels." Many cultures use fennel and fennel seed in their cookery, and they are common ingredients in Italian sausage and German rye bread. It is also one of the aromatic spices in Chinese five spice.

Beet Piquant Salad with Blood Oranges, Avocados, and Pistachios

Tired of the same worn-out beet salad with goat cheese and walnuts? Then this is for you! Kumquat Piquant Sauce serves as the base for the vinaigrette, and balsamic vinegar rounds out the dressing's flavor. Creamy avocados, juicy blood oranges, and toasted pistachios add a variety of textures alongside the fresh beets.

Serves 2 to 4

To make the vinaigrette, mix Kumquat Piquant Sauce, vinegar, and oil, and blend well.

To serve, plate the greens and top with avocado, oranges, and beets. Dress salad and garnish with toasted pistachios.

Vinaigrette

½ cup Kumquat Piquant Sauce (page 14)

3 tablespoons balsamic vinegar

2 tablespoons extra virgin olive oil

Greens

4 large handfuls mixed greens

1 avocado, sliced

1 blood orange, peeled and sectioned

1 or more large fresh beets, peeled and shredded (or use a spiralizer, if you have one)

¼ cup toasted pistachios

KUMQUAT RASPBERRY LAYERED GEL

There's something comforting about a bowl of Jell-O, perhaps because it's such a throwback to the '50s and '60s, when life seemed a lot simpler. This updated version is great with game or fowl. If you're over 50, I'm sure some version of this was on your family's table when you were growing up. And if you're too young to have experienced Jell-O salad before, this just might create a new memory for you.

Serves 6 to 8

1 cup boiling water

1 (3-ounce) package raspberry flavored gelatin

¼ cup Kumquat Conserve (page 14)

¼ cup cold water

1 (3-ounce) package cream cheese

¼ cup good-quality mayonnaise

¾ cup chopped pecans

½ cup confectioners' sugar

1 cup heavy cream, whipped

FInishing Touches

Sliced fresh kumquats

Pecan halves

Lightly coat 1 (2-quart) mold or 8 (8-ounce) individual molds with nonstick spray.

To prepare the gelatin, place boiling water in a small bowl. Sprinkle gelatin over the top, stirring gently to make sure all the granules are moistened and begin to dissolve. Cool for 15 minutes. Add the Kumquat Conserve (remove any stray seeds) and cold water. Mix thoroughly until gelatin completely dissolves. Pour into prepared mold or molds, leaving room for the second layer. To set, refrigerate for about 2 hours.

In a bowl, mix cream cheese, mayonnaise, chopped pecans, sugar, and whipped cream. Smoothly spread the mixture on top of the firm gelatin still in the mold(s). Refrigerate again until the cheese mixture is firm, at least 1 hour.

To serve, dip mold(s) into a slightly hot water bath to loosen and invert onto plates or serving dish. Garnish with fresh sliced kumquats and pecan halves. Voila!

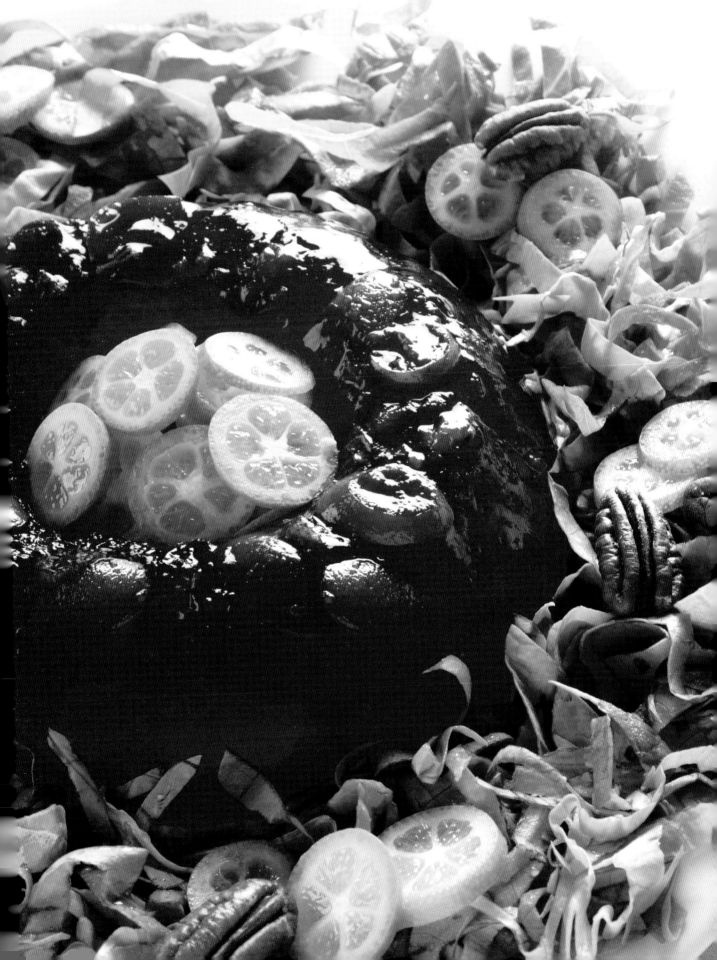

KUMQUAT-MARINATED CHINESE CHICKEN PANCAKES

Chestnut or water chestnut flour may be a new ingredient to you. In Asian cooking, it is used as a thickening agent much as American cooks would use cornstarch. You can find it online or at specialty markets. This recipe calls for half water chestnut flour and half all-purpose flour, but you can easily substitute cornstarch for the water chestnut flour.

Serves 6 to 8

To make the marinade, combine 1 cup Kumquat Piquant Sauce, soy sauce, sugar, rice wine, ginger, sweet pickle juice, salt, garlic, sesame oil, and chicken in a flat glass or plastic container. If needed, thin Kumquat Piquant Sauce with a little water or blood orange juice. Marinate for 30 minutes.

To prepare the pancake batter, place beaten eggs, flours, peas, and ¾ cup nuts in a large bowl. Remove chicken from marinade and add to batter. Gently fold all ingredients together.

To cook the pancakes, place 1 to 2 tablespoons oil in a hot skillet and pour in enough batter to make pancake of desired size. Fry until bubbles appear on top. Flip pancake and cook for another 1 to 2 minutes, just until chicken is done. Drain on paper towels. Repeat with remaining batter.

To serve, plate pancakes, drizzle with remaining Kumquat Piquant Sauce, and garnish with additional chopped nuts, if desired.

Marinade

1½ cups Kumquat Piquant Sauce (page 14), divided

2 to 3 tablespoons soy sauce

1 teaspoon granulated sugar

1 tablespoon rice wine

1 teaspoon crushed fresh ginger

1 teaspoon sweet pickle juice (juice from a jar of gherkins) or sweet Asian sauce

¾ teaspoon salt

1 teaspoon crushed fresh garlic

½ teaspoon toasted sesame oil

1 (4- to 5-pound) whole chicken, skinned, deboned, and chopped into small chunks

Batter

3 eggs, beaten

½ cup water chestnut flour or cornstarch

½ cup unbleached all-purpose flour

¾ cup fresh peas

1 cup coarsely chopped roasted peanuts, divided

Peanut oil, for frying

Hawaiian Chicken with Kumquats

Very quick and easy! Here's another one of those 10- to 15-minute recipes where you mix everything together and pop in the oven. If you like chicken in a sweet sauce, this is a winner, and kids seem to enjoy it, probably because of its sweet tang. This is a great potluck dish — just cut the chicken into chunks instead of baking the breasts whole.
People will ask you for the recipe.

Serves 4

¼ cup light brown sugar

½ cup ketchup

¼ cup red wine or apple cider vinegar

2 tablespoons cornstarch

1 small red bell pepper, seeded and chopped

1 cup pineapple chunks with juice, fresh or canned

8 or 9 kumquats, sliced

4 boneless and skinless chicken breast halves

Preheat oven to 375°F and position a rack in the center of the oven.

Mix all ingredients except chicken in a bowl. Place chicken in a casserole or baking dish, pour sauce over the chicken, and cover with foil. Bake for approximately 20 minutes or until the chicken is fully cooked.

Serve with rice or noodles.

KUMQUAT CHICKEN KEBABS
WITH BLOOD ORANGE DIPPING SAUCE

You'll find yourself savoring every last drop of this creamy citrus dipping sauce.
It's memorable! Try this with lean pork, too.

Serves 4 to 6

Preheat grill to medium-high or preheat broiler. If using bamboo skewers, soak them in water for at least 2 hours before using to prevent burning.

To prepare the marinade, combine oil, Kumquat Purée, blood orange juice, ginger, and chicken in a flat glass dish or plastic container. Marinate chicken, refrigerated, for at least 2 hours or up to 24 hours. When ready to cook, thread cubes onto skewers and reserve marinade.

To make the dipping sauce, place marinade in a medium saucepan over medium heat. Bring to a boil and stir in sugar. Lower heat and simmer gently until slightly reduced, about 20 minutes. Stir in heavy cream and swirl in butter at the end. If the sauce is too thick, thin to desired consistency with extra blood orange juice. Season with salt and pepper.

To cook the meat, lightly coat chicken kebabs with olive oil. Cook on the grill or under the broiler, basting with marinade, until done.

Serve with dipping sauce on the side.

Marinade

⅓ cup extra virgin olive oil

2 cups Kumquat Purée (page 14)

1½ cups blood orange juice, plus extra as needed (about 7-8 large blood oranges)

½ teaspoon ginger powder or 1 (1-inch) piece fresh peeled and grated ginger

4 boneless and skinless chicken breast halves, or 2 pounds lean pork, cubed

Olive oil or vegetable oil, for brushing skewers

Dipping Sauce

½ cup granulated sugar

½ cup heavy cream

2 tablespoons salted butter

Salt and freshly ground black pepper, to taste

KUMQUAT-GLAZED CHICKEN WITH BOK CHOY

Here's another easy dinner that you can whip up in minutes.
If you start the rice just before you cook the chicken, everything will be ready
in less than 30 minutes.

Serves 4

2 tablespoons liquid from Kumquat Conserve (page 14)

2 teaspoons sherry vinegar

2 to 4 tablespoons vegetable oil, divided

4 chicken thighs, skin on

1 clove garlic, finely diced

8 bunches baby bok choy, halved or quartered

Salt and freshly ground black pepper, to taste

Finishing Touch

Kumquat halves from Kumquat Conserve

Your favorite rice

To make the glaze, mix liquid from Kumquat Conserve and vinegar in a small bowl. Set aside.

To cook the chicken, heat 1 to 2 tablespoons oil in a skillet over medium-high and sauté thighs until done. Transfer to a heatproof platter, brush generously with glaze, and hold in a warm oven or cover with foil.

Add remaining oil and garlic to the same skillet and briefly sauté the bok choy over medium-high heat until just wilted. Season with salt and pepper.

Brush chicken with more glaze. Serve with bok choy and more kumquat halves from the Kumquat Conserve. Add your favorite rice.

GRILLED PORK MEDALLIONS WITH KUMQUAT VINAIGRETTE

If you haven't used rubs for meats, now is the time to try one. A rub is simple and quick to make, and you'll find it greatly enhances meat. The sesame seeds add a slight nutty touch, and the black pepper and cayenne give the dish a little kick.

Serves 4 to 6

Rub

3 tablespoons black
    peppercorns

2 tablespoons white or black
    sesame seeds

½ teaspoon cayenne pepper

2 teaspoons salt

3 cloves garlic, minced

1 (1½-pound) pork
    tenderloin, cut into
    1½-inch rounds

Vinaigrette

¼ cup apple cider vinegar

2 tablespoons fresh lemon
    juice

1 tablespoon Dijon mustard

2 tablespoons minced
    shallots

½ cup olive oil

½ cup Kumquat Conserve
    (page 14)

Salt and freshly ground
    pepper, to taste

Greens

8 cups baby spinach

1 (11-ounce) can Mandarin
    oranges, drained, or
    segments from 1 to 2 fresh
    blood oranges

¼ cup thinly sliced red onion

½ cup crumbled blue cheese

4 to 6 fresh kumquats, sliced

Preheat grill to medium-high. Lightly oil the grill just before using.

To make the rub, grind the peppercorns and sesame seeds in a food processor or coffee grinder until coarse. Transfer to a small bowl and stir in cayenne, salt, and garlic. Cover the pork liberally with the rub, patting it into the meat. Refrigerate until ready to cook.

To make the vinaigrette, lightly pulse the first four vinaigrette ingredients in a food processor. Drizzle in the olive oil until the dressing emulsifies. Stir in Kumquat Conserve and season with salt and pepper. Set aside.

To cook the pork, grill the tenderloin until just pink inside, about 3 minutes per side, or until meat registers 145°F on an instant-read thermometer. Transfer pork to a platter and cover.

In a large bowl, dress spinach with just enough vinaigrette to lightly coat the leaves. Toss in orange segments, onion, blue cheese, and fresh kumquat slices. Plate salad and top with pork medallions. Drizzle each serving with additional dressing.

Pork Loin with Rice Stuffing and Kumquat Glaze

Perfect for a family gathering, this luscious pork roast is filled with a rice stuffing laden with toasted pine nuts and basted with flavorful Kumquat Piquant Sauce.

Serves 6 to 8

1 tablespoon unsalted butter

¼ cup pine nuts

2 tablespoons minced white onion

1½ cups uncooked rice (use your favorite)

1 cup chicken stock

1 cup water

Salt and freshly ground black pepper, to taste

1 tablespoon chopped fresh cilantro leaves

½ cup chopped kumquat halves from Kumquat Conserve (page 14)

1 (4- to 5-pound) pork loin, butterflied

Salt and freshly ground black pepper, to taste

1 to 2 tablespoons vegetable oil

½ cup Kumquat Piquant Sauce (page 14)

Finishing Touches

2 teaspoons chopped fresh parsley or cilantro leaves

Kumquat Piquant Sauce (page 14)

Preheat oven to 400°F.

Melt butter in an ovenproof skillet on low heat and add pine nuts. Brown slightly. Remove nuts and set aside. In the same pan, add onions and cook until soft. Stir rice into the onion mixture; add stock, water, salt and pepper, and cilantro. Bring to a boil over moderate heat. Cover, reduce heat to low, and simmer for approximately 20 minutes, or until tender. At the end, stir in toasted pine nuts and kumquat pieces.

Place the meat on work surface with the short end parallel to the edge of the work surface. Season with salt and pepper. Spread with only enough rice to allow you to tightly roll the loin, leaving about an inch uncovered at the edge. Reserve remaining rice to be served as a side dish. Roll the loin very tightly away from you toward the end with no rice. Tightly secure with kitchen twine.

Using the same skillet, add vegetable oil and heat on high. Sear the loin until golden brown on all sides, about 2 to 3 minutes per side. Transfer the skillet to the oven and roast the loin until an instant-read thermometer inserted into the center of the meat registers 140°F to 150°F, about 30 to 35 minutes. At 15 minutes, glaze pork with Kumquat Piquant Sauce. When done, let pork rest 15 to 20 minutes before cutting into ½-inch slices.

Plate pork slices with remaining rice, sprinkle with parsley or cilantro, and serve with Kumquat Piquant Sauce on the side.

KUMQUAT PASTA WITH HAZELNUTS

Okay, so you're thinking, kumquats and pasta? Yes! They are great together, along with a nutty side note of hazelnuts that round out this dish. Simple, easy, and yummy, this is a great quick wintertime dinner when kumquats are fresh and in season. It's also great as a pasta salad.

Serves 4

Preheat oven to 350°F and position a rack in the center of the oven.

Place hazelnuts on a sheet pan and toast in the oven until the skins come off easily, about 10 to 15 minutes. Roll the nuts in a cloth or between your hands to remove as much of the skin as possible. Coarsely chop the nuts and set aside.

Cook dried pasta to al dente, according to package instructions, or if using fresh pasta, bring a large pot of salted water to boil over high heat and add a little oil and the fresh pasta. Cook until tender but still firm to the bite, stirring occasionally, about 4 to 5 minutes.

When the pasta is ready, drain it, return it to the pot, and quickly toss with oil as desired, pea pods, parsley, salt to taste, and chopped hazelnuts. Plate the pasta and sprinkle with kumquat slices. Serve immediately.

1 cup whole hazelnuts

1 pound dried or fresh gemelli or your favorite pasta

¼ to ½ cup hazelnut or walnut oil (available at specialty markets or online)

1 cup pea pods, quickly blanched, and cut in half diagonally

¼ cup finely chopped Italian parsley leaves

Salt, to taste

16 fresh kumquats, thinly sliced and seeded

KUMQUAT COCONUT SPONGE CAKE

Baking a good sponge cake requires a bit of patience because it is a multi-step procedure, but I can promise you it is totally worth it. Queen Victoria used to enjoy sponge cake layered with raspberry and whipped cream with her afternoon tea. For the best results, assemble the cake a day ahead and refrigerate before serving so the flavors have a chance to meld.

Makes 1

Syrup

½ cup water

½ cup granulated sugar

½ cup Kumquat Purée
(page 14)

Batter

5 large eggs, separated

1¼ cups plus 3 tablespoons
granulated sugar, divided

⅓ cup Kumquat Purée
(page 14)

1 teaspoon pure vanilla
paste or extract

1½ cups sifted cake flour

½ teaspoon baking powder

¼ teaspoon salt ››

Cooking tip: *Because the cake is supported by air bubbles whipped into the batter, don't remove it from the oven until is it done baking; otherwise, it may lose some of its air and flatten.*

Preheat oven to 350°F and position a rack in the center of the oven. Line the bottom of a round 9x3-inch cake pan with parchment paper. Do not grease the sides.

To make the syrup, place all syrup ingredients in a small saucepan. Bring to a boil, reduce heat, and simmer for 10 minutes. Pour through a fine-mesh strainer into a bowl and press firmly to remove as much liquid as possible, discarding the solids. You should have about ⅔ cup syrup. Chill until needed.

To make the batter, place the egg yolks and 1¼ cups of sugar in the bowl of a stand mixer fitted with the whisk attachment. Whip on high speed until the mixture is thick and very light in color and flows in ribbons off a spoon. Scrape down the bowl and whip in the Kumquat Purée and vanilla. In a separate ››

ABOUT SPONGE CAKE

The sponge cake is thought to be one of the oldest cakes baked without yeast. The earliest record appears to be an English poem written in 1615. A sponge cake is firm and well-aerated, similar to a sea sponge. Since it has no yeast, the batter recipe often calls for adding baking powder and whipping the eggs and sugar to a thick, light consistency. Around the world, there are many kinds of sponge cake — in the U.S. it can also be known as a chiffon cake, in France the genoise, and in Latin America the tres leches cake. Sponge cakes are also popular during Passover, when matzo meal is used instead of flour.

‹‹ bowl, sift together cake flour, baking powder, and salt. Fold this into the batter, stirring until no streaks remain. Set aside. In a clean bowl of the stand mixer fitted with a clean whisk attachment, whip the egg whites to soft peaks. Then slowly whip in the remaining 3 tablespoons of sugar until smooth. Carefully fold the egg white mixture into the batter and pour into the prepared pan. Bake for 40 to 50 minutes, or until the top of the cake is golden brown and the center is firm to the touch. It's okay if the center of the cake falls a bit. Place pan on a rack to cool completely.

To make the coconut pastry cream filling, mix cornstarch and 2 tablespoons milk in a small bowl until smooth. Set aside. Place the yolks in a separate small bowl and stir to blend. In a medium saucepan, stir ⅔ cup milk, sugar, and vanilla bean, and heat until scalded. Whisk in the cornstarch mixture and blend well. Slowly pour egg yolks into the saucepan and cook over medium heat, whisking constantly, until the mixture comes to a boil and thickens. Cook for 1 minute. Remove from the heat and whisk in butter until completely blended. Pour through a fine-mesh strainer into a clean bowl and stir in coconut and cardamom.

Place a piece of plastic wrap directly on the surface of the pastry cream and cool completely. Refrigerate until needed.

To make the whipped cream frosting, whip all ingredients together in a stand mixer fitted with whisk attachment until firm peaks form. Refrigerate until needed.

To assemble, remove the cake from the pan and trim the top to level the cake. Slice the cake in half to form two layers. Place the top cake layer on a cake cardboard or serving plate. Brush 3 tablespoons of kumquat syrup over the surface. Evenly spread the cold pastry cream filling on top. Brush the cut surface of the second cake layer with 3 tablespoons of kumquat syrup. Invert the cake on top of the filling. Remove the parchment paper and brush the top of the cake with an additional 3 tablespoons of kumquat syrup. Frost the top and sides of cake with the whipped cream frosting.

To finish, press the coconut into the top and sides of the cake, completely covering it in an even layer. Evenly space a ring of kumquat halves around the bottom of the cake. Refrigerate until ready to serve. For the best results, assemble the cake a day ahead and refrigerate so the flavors have a chance to meld.

Coconut Pastry Cream Filling

2½ tablespoons cornstarch

⅔ cup plus 2 tablespoons whole milk, divided

4 large egg yolks

1 cup granulated sugar

½ vanilla bean, split and scraped

2 tablespoons unsalted butter, cut into 4 pieces

½ cup unsweetened dried shredded coconut

Pinch ground cardamom

Whipped Cream Frosting

3 cups heavy cream

5 tablespoons granulated sugar

1½ teaspoons pure vanilla extract

Finishing Touches

1¾ cups unsweetened dried large-flake coconut, toasted

Kumquat halves from Kumquat Conserve (page 14)

Kumquat Cranberry Almond Upside Down Cake

Here's a refreshing take on the traditional pineapple upside down cake where kumquats stand in for pineapple and cranberries for cherries. I have always hated those overly sweet, artificially colored cherries anyway. Yum!

Makes 1

Topping

4 tablespoons unsalted butter

½ cup packed light brown sugar

18 fresh kumquats, sliced in half and seeded

1 cup fresh cranberries

Batter

6 ounces almond paste, room temperature, cut into ½-inch pieces

½ cup granulated sugar

½ cup (1 stick) unsalted butter, room temperature

1 teaspoon pure vanilla extract

3 large eggs, room temperature

½ cup plus 2 tablespoons unbleached all-purpose flour

¾ teaspoon baking powder

Pinch salt

Preheat oven to 350°F and position a rack in the center of the oven. Lightly coat a 9x1½-inch round cake pan with nonstick spray.

To make the topping, melt butter and brown sugar in a small saucepan over low heat. When it is hot and liquefied, pour it into the prepared cake pan and tilt the pan so that the mixture covers the bottom in a thin layer. Arrange kumquat halves evenly in the pan, placing them cut side up. (The round, skin side is much prettier and should face the bottom of the pan). Fill in the spaces between the kumquats with the cranberries. Gently push all of the fruit into the brown sugar mixture. Set aside.

To make the batter, place almond paste and sugar in the bowl of a food processor and pulse until smooth, about 20 seconds. Add softened butter and pulse until well combined, about 30 seconds. Add vanilla and pulse again. Add eggs one at a time, allowing each one to blend in before adding the next. In a small bowl, combine flour, baking powder, and salt. Add dry ingredients to the food processor and blend well, about 20 seconds. Scrape the batter into the cake pan and gently spread it to completely cover the fruit. It will seem like there is not enough batter. Bake for 50 minutes, or until golden brown and a cake tester inserted into the center comes out clean. Place pan on a rack to cool for 10 minutes.

To serve, run a thin knife or spatula around the edge of the pan to release the cake and invert it onto a plate. Serve warm or at room temperature.

KUMQUAT GINGER AND BLOOD ORANGE ROULADE WITH WHITE CHOCOLATE CREAM

I have a thing for roulades, or rolled cakes. The most familiar version in the United States is the jellyroll. In the persimmon chapter, I included a Persimmon Walnut Roulade, and now I'm introducing you to a Kumquat Ginger Roulade. Roulades look impressive, but they're simple to make. It is a sponge cake, beaten full of air to give it lightness. This is why it is easy to roll.

Makes 1 roulade, enough to serve 8 to 10

Preheat oven to 375°F and position a rack in the center of the oven. Line a 12x18x1-inch jellyroll pan with parchment paper.

To make the kumquat ginger curd, bring 2 inches of water to a boil in the bottom of a double boiler, then lower heat to a simmer. In the top of the double boiler, off the heat, whisk the Kumquat Ginger Syrup, lime juice, and sugar. Add the egg yolks and continue whisking until well combined. Set the top of the double boiler back over the simmering water in the bottom pan and cook the curd, whisking constantly, until it becomes very thick and holds a slight shape on the surface and registers about 175°F to 180°F on an instant-read thermometer. Do not let the mixture boil or the eggs will scramble. Remove from the heat and pour through a fine-mesh strainer into a clean bowl. Whisk in butter until completely melted and blended into the curd. Place a piece of plastic wrap directly on the surface of the curd to keep a skin from forming and refrigerate until needed. If you are making the cake immediately, place the curd over an ice bath to chill quickly. The curd can be made 2 days in advance.

To make the batter, bring 2 inches of water to a boil in a medium saucepan, then lower heat to a simmer. Place the eggs and sugar in the bowl of a stand mixer and set the bowl over the simmering water. Whisk constantly until the eggs are hot to the touch and the sugar dissolves. Take the bowl off the heat. Place it in the stand mixer fitted with the whisk attachment and whip on high speed until the egg mixture cools, thickens, becomes very light in color, and triples in volume, about 4 to 5 minutes. In a separate bowl, sift together the cake flour, cardamom, and salt, whisking until blended. Take the bowl out of the stand mixer, and sift and gently fold the dry ingredients into the beaten eggs in 2 or 3 additions. In a separate bowl, stir the orange zest into the melted butter, add a large spoonful of the cake batter, and blend well. Pour this mixture back into ›› »

Kumquat Ginger Curd

1 cup Kumquat Ginger Syrup (page 14)

2 tablespoons fresh lime juice

½ cup granulated sugar

6 large egg yolks, room temperature

6 tablespoons unsalted butter, cold and cut into ½-inch pieces

Batter

4 large eggs

⅔ cup granulated sugar

¾ cup sifted cake flour

½ teaspoon ground cardamom

½ teaspoon salt

1 blood orange, zested

6 tablespoons unsalted butter, melted until lukewarm but still fluid

White Chocolate Cream Frosting

7 ounces good quality white chocolate (I prefer Tobler or Lindt)

¼ cup water

1¼ cups heavy cream

Finishing Touch

Kumquat halves from Kumquat Conserve (page 14)

‹‹ the bowl of batter, and gently but quickly fold it in, just until blended and no streaks of butter remain. Spread the batter evenly onto the prepared jellyroll pan. Bake for 10 minutes, or until the center springs back when gently pressed with a fingertip and the top is golden brown. Place pan on a rack to cool completely.

To assemble the roulade, run a small knife or spatula around the edge of the pan to release the cooled cake. Invert it onto a large sheet of parchment or wax paper, and make sure the long edges of the cake are parallel to you and the edge of your work surface. Peel off the piece of parchment on the bottom of the cake. Spread the cooled curd over the cake in an even layer, leaving a ½-inch margin at the long edge farthest from you. Beginning with the edge closest to you, roll the cake, tucking and tightening as you go, into a long log, ending with the top edge of the cake on the bottom of the roll to ensure that the cake does not unroll during storage or serving. Transfer the roulade to a serving platter or cake cardboard, cover with plastic, and refrigerate until the white chocolate cream is ready.

To make the white chocolate cream frosting, bring 2 inches of water to a boil in the bottom of the double boiler, then turn off the heat. Place the chocolate and water in the top pan of the double boiler and set it over the simmering water in the bottom pan. Stir the mixture frequently until the chocolate is completely melted and smooth. Remove the top pan from the heat and set aside until the chocolate is cool to the touch and registers 85°F on an instant-read thermometer. If the chocolate is even a little too warm, it will cause the whipped cream to break and ruin the frosting. In the bowl of a stand mixer fitted with the whisk attachment, whip the cream to soft peaks, then gently fold the cooled chocolate mixture into the cream. It will seem soft at first, but it will quickly thicken and begin to harden.

To finish the roulade, quickly spread the white chocolate cream over the cake roll, covering the ends as well. Refrigerate until ready to serve.

KUMQUAT AND BLOOD ORANGE MASCARPONE LAYER CAKE

This festive cake is lightly scented with orange, moistened with kumquat syrup,
frosted with a rich mascarpone icing, and topped with a kumquat gelee
that makes the top of the cake shimmer. Gorgeous and luscious!

Makes 1

Preheat oven to 325°F and position a rack in the center of the oven. Line two 9x2-inch round cake pans with parchment paper. Do not grease the sides.

To make the kumquat syrup, place all syrup ingredients in a small saucepan. Bring to a boil, reduce heat, and simmer for 10 minutes. Pour through a fine-mesh strainer into a bowl and press firmly to remove as much liquid as possible, discarding the solids. You should have about 1¼ to 1½ cups syrup. Chill until ready to use in the batter, to moisten the layers of cake, in the filling and frosting, and in the gelee.

To make the batter, sift cake flour, 3 tablespoons sugar, baking powder, and salt into a large bowl. Mix well. Stir in oil, egg yolks, kumquat syrup, orange juice, and zest. Place the egg whites and cream of tartar in the bowl of a stand mixer fitted with the whisk attachment, and whip to soft peaks. Slowly add the remaining sugar and continue to whip until firm, moist peaks form (they should not be stiff). Fold egg whites into the batter until no streaks remain. Divide the batter between the cake pans and bake for 27 to 30 minutes, or until the tops of the cakes are golden brown and the centers are firm to the touch. Place pans on a rack to cool completely.

To make the filling and frosting, combine mascarpone, sugar, vanilla, and 2 tablespoons heavy cream in a medium bowl. Gently stir to blend just until smooth. Do not over-mix or mascarpone will become grainy. In the bowl of a stand mixer fitted with the whisk attachment, whip the remaining cream to soft peaks. Stir ⅓ whipped cream into mascarpone; then fold in the remaining cream. Transfer ⅓ of this mixture to a small bowl and stir in the minced kumquat halves and kumquat syrup. This will be the filling. The remaining mascarpone-whipped cream mixture will be the frosting.

To assemble, invert the first cake onto a serving plate, and remove the parchment paper. Brush ¼ cup kumquat syrup over the top. Next, spread filling in an even layer. »

Kumquat Syrup

1 cup water

1 cup granulated sugar

1 cup Kumquat Purée (page 14)

Batter

1 cup plus 2 tablespoons sifted cake flour

6 tablespoons granulated sugar, divided

1½ teaspoons baking powder

½ teaspoon salt

¼ cup vegetable oil

3 large eggs, separated, plus 1 extra egg white

¼ cup kumquat syrup

½ cup blood orange juice

½ large blood orange, zested

¼ teaspoon cream of tartar

Filling and Frosting

8 ounces mascarpone cheese

3 tablespoons granulated sugar

1 teaspoon pure vanilla extract or paste

4 cups heavy cream, divided

½ cup minced kumquat halves from Kumquat Conserve (page 14)

1 tablespoon kumquat syrup

Gelee

¼ cup kumquat syrup

¼ heaping teaspoon powdered unflavored gelatin

<< Invert second cake on top of the filling. Brush with ¼ cup kumquat syrup. Cover the top and sides of the cake with frosting. Transfer the remaining frosting to a pastry bag fitted with a ½-inch star tip. Pipe a border of reverse shells or any pattern you like around the top edge of the cake. Refrigerate cake while you prepare the gelee.

To make the gelee, pour syrup into a small bowl, sprinkle gelatin over the top and stir gently to make sure all the granules are moistened. Let sit for 5 minutes. Place the small bowl in a larger bowl of hot, but not boiling, water, and stir mixture until the liquid warms and the gelatin completely dissolves. Let the mixture cool until just lukewarm. Remove cake from refrigerator and pour gelee into the center of the top. Pick the cake up and gently tilt it so that the gelee distributes evenly, all the way to the piped border. To set, refrigerate at least 1 hour.

Assemble and refrigerate the cake a day before serving so the flavors can meld.

When ready to serve, slice the cake with a warm knife, wiping clean after each cut so gelee doesn't stick to the knife.

Kumquat Swirl Cheesecake

My favorite line in any recipe: "Do not let the mixture boil or the eggs will scramble."
Sounds funny, but if you've ever done it, you weren't laughing. So don't say you weren't
forewarned. All joking aside, my niece has always said, "I love a cheesecake!"
so I developed this one for her. The swirls make it so very pretty.

Makes 1

Preheat oven to 325°F and position a rack in the center of the oven.

To make the ginger curd, bring 2 inches of water to a boil in the bottom of the double boiler, then lower heat to a simmer. In the top of the double boiler, off the heat, whisk together the Kumquat Ginger Syrup and lime juice. Add egg yolks and sugar and whisk well. Set the top of the double boiler over the pan with the simmering water and cook the curd, whisking constantly, until it is very thick and coats the back of a spoon, about 170°F on an instant instant-read thermometer. Do not let the mixture boil or eggs will scramble. Remove from heat and pour through a fine-mesh strainer into a clean bowl. Add butter and whisk until it has completely melted and blended into the curd. Place a piece of plastic wrap directly on the surface of the curd to keep a skin from forming and refrigerate until needed. If you are making the cake immediately, place the curd over an ice bath to chill quickly. The curd can be made 2 days in advance.

To make the filling, cut cream cheese into pieces and place in the food processor. Add sugar and process, scraping down the sides several times, until the mixture is very, very smooth. Add the egg and egg yolk and process until well blended.

To assemble, pour the cheesecake filling into the prepared crust. Pipe or spread the chilled curd over the top and drag the tip of a toothpick or a small, sharp knife through the curd to create a marbleized pattern.

To bake, place the cheesecake in the oven for 40 to 50 minutes, until the edges are firm and the very center still wiggles a bit when the pan is gently shaken. Place pie on a rack to cool completely at room temperature, then refrigerate for at least 2 more hours before serving.

Ginger Curd
⅓ cup plus 1 tablespoon Kumquat Ginger Syrup (page 14)

1 tablespoon fresh lime juice

2 large egg yolks

⅓ cup granulated sugar

2 tablespoons unsalted butter

Filling
2 (8-ounce) packages cream cheese

¾ cup plus 2 tablespoons granulated sugar

1 large egg

1 large egg yolk

Crust
1 pre-made graham cracker pie crust (page 57)

ROMAN CHEESE CAKE WITH RICOTTA, KUMQUATS, AND CHOCOLATE

Cheesecake 101: Before you go any further, there is one very important thing you should know. A Roman cheese cake is actually a cheese cake — cheese baked into a cake. It can also be a kind of a cheese tart with a pastry top — nothing like what you imagine when you think "cheesecake."

Makes 1

Crust

2½ cups unbleached all-purpose flour

½ cup granulated sugar

¼ teaspoon salt

1 cup (2 sticks) cold, unsalted butter, cut into ½-inch pieces

4 large egg yolks

1 tablespoon pure vanilla extract

2 to 3 teaspoons water, as needed

Filling

1 (15-ounce) container whole milk or low-fat ricotta cheese

½ cup granulated sugar

2 large eggs

1 blood orange, zested

1 lemon, zested

½ cup Kumquat Conserve (page 14)

2 tablespoons grated semisweet chocolate

To make the crust, place flour, sugar, and salt in the bowl of a food processor and pulse for 10 seconds, until well combined. Add cold butter and pulse until the mixture resembles coarse crumbs. Divide dough evenly into 2 round disks. At this point, you can securely wrap the disks of dough and freeze them for up to 1 month.

To continue, place each piece of dough between 2 sheets of plastic wrap or wax paper. Roll each piece into a large circle, about 11 inches across. As you roll, the plastic will wrinkle; when this happens, peel it off and replace it smoothly over dough, then flip the dough over and repeat with the plastic on the other side before you continue rolling. Leave one of the rolled-out crusts between the plastic layers and transfer it onto a sheet pan.

Take the second rolled-out crust and place it on a 9- or 9½-inch fluted tart pan with a removable bottom or a fluted ceramic tart dish. To do this, remove the top piece of plastic, then lift the dough by the bottom plastic and flip it over into the tart pan, centering it as best you can. Peel off the remaining layer of plastic. Press the dough into the tart pan using your fingertips and trimming any excess dough from the edges. Patch any tears by pressing dough together with your fingertips. Place the tart pan on top of the plastic-wrapped dough already on the sheet pan and place the sheet pan in the refrigerator for 1 hour.

Preheat oven to 375°F and position a rack in the lower third of the oven. »

‹‹ Remove chilled tart pan from refrigerator, but leave the flat dough on the sheet pan in the refrigerator. Line the chilled tart shell with a piece of foil, pressing it firmly into the corners of the pan. Fill the pan with pie weights, rice, or beans. Bake for about 15 minutes, or until the edges and center are set and no longer stick to the foil when you try to lift it off. Place crust on a rack to cool completely.

To make the filling, place ricotta and sugar in the bowl of a food processor and pulse until very smooth. Add eggs and pulse again. Blend in orange and lemon zest. Add Kumquat Conserve and pulse until conserve is chopped but still chunky, about 3 to 5 seconds. Stir in the grated chocolate by hand.

To finish the cheesecake, pour the filling into the pre-baked and cooled tart shell. Remove the remaining piece of rolled dough from the refrigerator. Peel off the plastic from both sides and place dough on a lightly floured surface. Using a ruler as a guide, cut the dough into ¾-inch-thick strips. Arrange the strips about 1 inch apart over the filling in a criss-cross lattice pattern. Press the ends of the strips against the sides of the tart shell to seal. Bake at 350°F for 45 to 50 minutes, or until filling is puffy and pastry is cooked throughout and golden. Place pan on rack to cool. After about 15 to 20 minutes, slip off the rim of the pan. (It's harder to get it off once the tart has completely cooled.) Finish cooling then enjoy!

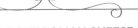

ABOUT ROMAN CHEESE CAKE

If this is your first encounter with Roman cheese cake, you may be fascinated by its ancient Greek history, which begins at least 4,000 years ago. Cheese had been made long before 2000 B.C., but without written history, we don't know exactly when it was first made. We do know that cheese cake was thought to provide energy and was fed to the Olympic athletes as far back as the first games in 776 B.C. This same cheese cake was also served as a wedding cake. Its humble ingredients were quite simple: flour, wheat, cheese, and honey.

When the Romans conquered Greece, they took the cheese cake with them. They modified the recipe by adding eggs and sometimes baking the filling in the dough rather than mixing all the ingredients together, as it was originally made.

As this cheese cake made its way throughout Europe, every culture put its own spin on it, including immigrants streaming into America. The early immigrant recipes eventually morphed into what we know today as cheesecake.

TRES LECHES CAKE WITH KUMQUATS, COCONUT, AND GINGER

Tres Leches Cake translates to English as "three milk cake." Traditionally the three milks are condensed, evaporated, and cream, and the cake usually doesn't contain butter, making it absorb more of the milks. I cheat a bit on the milk by using my Kumquat Ginger Syrup for the evaporated milk and coconut milk for the cream. The result is a tropical-inspired delight.

Makes 1

Batter

5 large eggs, separated

10 tablespoons granulated sugar, divided

1¼ cups sifted cake flour

½ cup packed sweetened flaked coconut, toasted

½ teaspoon baking powder

Milk Syrup

½ can (7 ounces) full-fat (not "lite") coconut milk

½ cup Kumquat Ginger Syrup (page 14)

¼ cup sweetened condensed milk

1 tablespoon fresh lime juice

Topping

1½ cups heavy cream

2 tablespoons granulated sugar, or to taste

Sweetened flaked coconut, toasted

Preheat oven to 350°F and position a rack in the center of the oven. Lightly grease a round 9x1½-inch cake pan.

To prepare the batter, place egg yolks and 5 tablespoons sugar in the bowl of a stand mixer fitted with the whisk attachment and beat on high until very light in color and thick, about 4 to 5 minutes. Place flour, coconut, and baking powder in a food processor and pulse until coconut is finely chopped. In a clean bowl and with a clean whisk attachment, beat egg whites on medium speed to soft peaks. With the mixer running, add the remaining sugar slowly and beat until the egg whites hold firm peaks. Fold one-third of egg whites into beaten yolks, and then fold in half of the dry mixture. Fold in half of the remaining whites and the rest of the dry mixture. Fold in the last of the egg whites until no streaks of white remain. Pour the batter into the prepared pan, level the top, and bake for 20 minutes, or until a cake tester inserted into the center comes out clean and the top is golden brown and feels firm to the touch. Place pan on a rack to cool for 10 minutes.

To finish the cake, make the milk syrup by combining milk syrup ingredients in a bowl. Poke a toothpick or skewer repeatedly into the top of the cake, and pour half of the milk syrup over the surface. Continue to poke the toothpick into the cake, all the way to the bottom of the pan, to help the syrup soak in. Tap the cake on the work surface a few times. When most of the milk syrup is absorbed, pour about half of the remaining liquid over the top and continue to poke and tap. Some liquid will remain on top of the cake; this is fine. Refrigerate at least 4 hours, or overnight is fine. Save leftover milk syrup for plating.

To make the topping, whip the cream and sugar to firm peaks. Invert the cake onto a serving plate and spoon milk syrup over and around the cake. Finish with whipped cream and toasted coconut.

VICTORIAN KUMQUAT BLOOD ORANGE CAKE

This heavy, moist English-style cake is best after resting for 24 hours. I much prefer it to a fruitcake because it tastes so good and isn't laden with over-sweet candied fruit.

Makes 1

Preheat oven to 325°F and position a rack in the center of the oven. Lightly coat a 9- or 10-inch springform pan with nonstick spray.

To make the batter, process orange peel, Kumquat Conserve, and raisins in a food processor until coarsely chopped. Set aside. In the bowl of a stand mixer fitted with the paddle attachment, cream sugar and butter. Add eggs and buttermilk and beat until well combined. In another bowl, sift flour, baking powder, baking soda, and salt, and stir in nuts. Fold flour mixture and chopped fruit into the creamed butter and sugar. Pour into the prepared springform pan. Bake for 45 minutes, or until cake is firm to the touch and a tester or toothpick inserted into the center comes out clean. Place pan on a rack to cool for 10 minutes.

To make the syrup, heat all the syrup ingredients in a small saucepan until sugar dissolves.

To finish, spoon syrup over the cake 1 tablespoon at a time. For best results, let cake flavors meld for at least 24 hours. Store in an airtight container or well wrapped at room temperature. Will keep for several days.

Batter

3 large blood oranges, peeled and juiced, reserve peel for batter and juice for syrup

¾ cup Kumquat Conserve (page 14)

1 cup raisins

1 cup granulated sugar

½ cup (1 stick) butter

2 eggs

¾ cup buttermilk

2 cups unbleached all-purpose flour

1 teaspoon baking powder

½ teaspoon baking soda

½ teaspoon salt

½ cup chopped nuts (use your favorite)

Syrup

1 cup blood orange juice

½ cup granulated sugar

1 tablespoon dark rum

Quick Kumquat Refrigerator Pie

Although I generally shun using products that aren't "natural," I will occasionally bend a bit. I prefer using heavy cream and whipping it myself, but when time is limited and I need a quick dessert, frozen whipped topping will work. This easy no-bake pie is cool and creamy, especially in the summer when you don't want to heat up your already too-hot kitchen.

Makes 1

1 (14-ounce) can sweetened condensed milk

⅔ cup Kumquat Purée (page 14)

½ cup fresh lime juice

1 (8-ounce) tub thawed Truwhip (available at specialty and natural food stores) or a good quality frozen whipped topping

1 (9-inch) store-bought or prebaked homemade chocolate pie crust (page 57)

Kumquat halves from Kumquat Conserve (page 14)

In the bowl of a stand mixer fitted with the whisk attachment, beat condensed milk, Kumquat Purée, and lime juice until thick. Fold in whipped topping. Pour into prepared pie shell and chill in refrigerator for several hours. Decorate with kumquat halves.

Kumquat Sour Cream Torte

This recipe is basically the same as the Persimmon Sour Cream Torte recipe on page 61 except that I've swapped the Persimmon Purée with Kumquat Purée. However, because of the nature of each fruit, the flavor is completely different. This delicious torte is composed of seven cookie-like layers, each with a kumquat sour cream filling. For the best results, refrigerate it for at least 5 hours, or even better, overnight, so the cookie layers soften and the flavors meld.

Makes 1

Preheat oven to 350°F and position a rack in the center of the oven. Lightly flour sheet pans.

To make the dough, place flour and sugar in a bowl and, using a pastry blender or two knives, work butter into flour mixture until it becomes soft and crumbly. Stir in egg. With your hands, mix until the dough sticks together, then divide into 7 equal parts. Roll each piece into a very thin 9-inch circle. You can leave the edges as is or use a 9-inch round plate as a guide to cut out the circles. Place the cookie circles on the prepared sheet pans.

Bake each circle for 10 to 12 minutes, or until the edges begin to brown lightly. Cool on sheet pans and carefully transfer to work surface. Repeat until all dough is baked.

To make the filling, mix all filling ingredients.

To assemble the torte, spread each cookie with filling and stack on a plate or cake pedestal. On top of the final layer, sprinkle remaining confectioners' sugar. Refrigerate for 5 hours or longer before serving.

Dough

3 cups sifted unbleached all-purpose flour

¾ cup granulated sugar

1 cup (2 sticks) unsalted butter

1 egg

Filling

2 cups finely chopped walnuts

2 cups sour cream

1½ cups confectioners' sugar

1 teaspoon pure ginger extract

⅔ cup Kumquat Purée (page 14)

Finishing Touch

Confectioners' sugar

Layered Kumquat Supreme Pie

*Here's another great chilled pie recipe and one of my personal favorites.
I love how the distinct sweet-tart citrus flavor of the kumquats come through.
This pie is best assembled and refrigerated overnight before serving.*

Makes 1 (9-inch) pie or 4 mini pies

Crust

1 unbaked homemade or
store-bought deep-dish
9-inch pastry shell

Kumquat Filling

1¼ cups granulated sugar

6 tablespoons cornstarch

½ teaspoon salt

1¼ cups cold water

2 tablespoons unsalted
butter

½ cup Kumquat Purée
(page 14)

Cream Cheese Filling

2 (8-ounce) packages cream
cheese, room temperature

¾ cup confectioners' sugar

1½ cups thawed Truwhip
(available at specialty
and natural food stores)
or a good quality frozen
whipped topping

2 tablespoons Kumquat
Purée (page 14)

Finishing Touch

Kumquat halves from
Kumquat Conserve

Preheat oven to 450°F and position a rack in the center of the oven.

To prepare the crust, line an unpricked pastry shell with a double thickness of foil. Bake for 8 minutes. Remove foil and bake 5 minutes longer. Place on a rack to cool.

To make the kumquat filling, combine sugar, cornstarch, salt, and cold water in a saucepan and stir, then place over medium heat and stir until sugar and cornstarch completely dissolve and mixture thickens, about 3 to 5 minutes.

Remove pan from heat and gently stir in butter and Kumquat Purée. Do not over-mix. Set aside to cool to room temperature, about 1 hour. Do not stir.

To make the cream cheese filling, in a stand mixer fitted with the paddle attachment, beat cream cheese and confectioners' sugar until smooth. Fold in whipped topping and Kumquat Purée. Transfer a half cup to a small bowl and refrigerate for garnishing.

To assemble, evenly spread the cream cheese mixture in the pie shell, then the kumquat filling. Chill overnight.

Keep refrigerated until ready to serve, then top with remaining mixture and kumquat halves.

KUMQUAT CHOP-CHOP COOKIES

Everyone asks the same question: Why are these called chop-chop cookies? Simple answer: because you do a lot of chopping. You'll chop the cookie dough with a cleaver as well as the candied ginger and pecans. And when it's all together and baked, you will have the most delightful bar cookies with a streusel topping. Chop chop!

Makes about 36

Preheat oven to 350°F and position a rack in the center of the oven.

To make the filling, gently combine all filling ingredients in a bowl, and set aside.

To make the dough, spread sugar on a large cutting board. Place the butter on top of the sugar and chop into small pieces with a cleaver. Gather together and make a well. Crack 1 egg into the well and chop with cleaver to combine. Make another well, crack the remaining egg into the well, and chop.

Sift together the remaining ingredients, spread over the top of the butter-sugar mixture, and chop again.

Pat half of the dough into a 12x18-inch jelly roll pan, evenly covering it. Spread filling on top. Sprinkle remaining dough over the filling. Bake for 35 minutes, or until golden brown. Cut into bars or for diamond-shape pieces cut into 3-inch squares and then cut each square diagonally. Store in an airtight container.

Filling

1¼ cups Kumquat Conserve (page 14)

1½ cups coarsely chopped candied or crystallized ginger

1½ cups coarsely chopped pecans (or your favorite nut)

Dough

2 cups granulated sugar

1 cup (2 sticks) unsalted butter, very firm and cold

2 large eggs

3½ cups unbleached all-purpose flour

2 teaspoons baking powder

Pinch salt

2 teaspoons powdered ginger

Kumquat Coconut Macaroons

These wonderful macaroons are crunchy on the outside and wonderfully creamy and sweet on the inside. I'm a fan of them right from the oven when the outside has a perfect crunch from the egg whites and the inside is still warm and gooey, but they are equally good at room temperature. They keep well in an airtight container and need not be refrigerated if you'll be eating them within a few days of baking — if they last that long!

Makes about 24

1¼ cups Kumquat Conserve (page 14)

1 cup granulated sugar

⅓ cup water

2 tablespoons fresh lime juice

3 cups unsweetened shredded dried coconut

3 large egg whites

In a food processor, pulse Kumquat Conserve until kumquat pieces are coarsely chopped. Set aside. In a medium saucepan, stir in sugar, water, and lime juice, and bring to a boil over medium heat. Turn the heat to low and cook, stirring frequently, until the mixture darkens a little, thickens, and reduces to about 1⅓ to 1¼ cups. Pour into the bowl of a stand mixer fitted with the paddle attachment. Add chopped conserve and coconut and beat on medium until well blended. Add egg whites one at a time, blending in each one thoroughly before adding the next. Place a piece of plastic wrap directly on the surface of the warm batter and refrigerate until cold. (The batter can be kept refrigerated for several days.)

When ready to bake, preheat oven to 350°F and position a rack in the center of the oven. Stack two sheet pans on top of each other and line the top pan with parchment paper.

Using an ice cream scoop or with your hands, shape the macaroon batter into cookies the size of golf balls and place on the prepared sheet pans. Bake for 23 to 28 minutes, or until golden brown on top, rotating the pans halfway through the baking time. Place sheet pans on rack to cool. These cookies are best the same day they are baked while they are crunchy on the outside and soft on the inside. If kept longer, the cookies lose their crispness, but are still delicious.

KUMQUAT GINGER RUGELACH

Rugelach are a Jewish pastry originating in Eastern Europe. Its name in Yiddish translates to "little twists," describing the shape of the cookie. In some American versions, cream cheese is used in the dough instead of sour cream, but the secret to a tender and flaky rugelach is the sour cream. I'm sure you've had rugelach with apricot, walnut, poppy seed, or chocolate fillings, but I'll bet you haven't had kumquats!

Makes about 24 pieces

To make the dough, pulse flour and salt in a food processor. Add butter and process until it resembles peas and cornmeal, about 10 to 15 pulses. In a small bowl, whisk egg yolk and sour cream. Add to the food processor and pulse until it resembles crumble topping, about 15 pulses. (It should not yet be a cohesive dough.) Turn out onto a work surface and knead gently several times, just until it comes together. Divide into 3 equal pieces and shape into 5-inch rounds. Cover in plastic wrap and refrigerate for 2 hours or overnight.

To make the filling, pulse kumquats and ginger in a food processor until a smooth paste forms. Transfer to a small bowl. In a separate small bowl, thoroughly mix sugar and cardamom.

Stack two ½-inch sided sheet pans on top of each other and line the top one with parchment paper. (This double-panning will prevent the bottoms of the cookies from getting too dark.)

To assemble, lightly flour work surface and roll 1 piece of dough into an 11-inch round about ⅛ inch thick. Spread with ⅓ of the kumquat paste, stopping ½ inch from the sides, and sprinkle ⅓ of the cardamom sugar and ⅓ of the nuts over the top. Cut round into 12 wedges. Roll each piece into a crescent — start at the wide end and roll tightly toward the point, ending with the point under each cookie. Place on prepared sheet pans and refrigerate for at 30 minutes to chill the dough before baking. Repeat as necessary.

Preheat oven to 350°F and position racks in the top and center third of the oven.

Sprinkle cookies with a little extra sugar or cardamom and bake for 30 to 35 minutes, or until nicely browned on the bottom and lightly golden on top. Reverse sheet pans from front to back and top to bottom racks halfway through baking. Cool and store in an airtight container.

Dough

2 cups unbleached all-purpose flour

½ teaspoon salt

½ cup (1 stick) cold butter, cut into ½-inch pieces

1 large egg yolk

¾ cup sour cream

Filling

1¼ cups kumquat halves from Kumquat Conserve (page 14)

¼ cup chopped candied ginger

9 tablespoons granulated sugar

½ teaspoon ground cardamom

¾ cup toasted and chopped almonds or cashews

KUMQUAT NAPOLEON

This is a quick and simple twist on a French Napoleon. You can make a delicious no-cook filling with four simple ingredients, but if you want the "real deal," make the pastry cream and use it instead. Either way, this is a lovely dessert that takes no time at all but looks like it did!

Makes 4

Pastry Cream Filling

1 cup whole milk

1 cup heavy cream

½ cup Kumquat Purée (page 14)

½ cup plus 2 tablespoons granulated sugar, divided

2 tablespoons unbleached all-purpose flour

1½ tablespoons cornstarch

2 large eggs plus 2 large egg yolks

3 tablespoons unsalted butter, cut into ½-inch pieces

Quick No-Cook Filling

1 (8-ounce) tub thawed Truwhip (available at specialty and natural food stores) or good quality frozen whipped topping

1 (14-ounce) can sweetened condensed milk

½ cup fresh lime juice

⅔ cup Kumquat Purée (page 14)

Dough

1 sheet frozen puff pastry, thawed and refrigerated until ready to use

Finishing Touch

Confectioners' sugar

To make the pastry cream filling, heat milk, cream, and Kumquat Purée in a saucepan over medium heat to just below the boiling point. In a bowl, whisk ½ cup sugar, flour, and cornstarch. When the milk mixture is hot, pour about ½ cup of it into the flour and whisk to blend well. Pour this back into the pan and whisk constantly to prevent lumps, until it comes to a boil and thickens.

In another bowl, whisk eggs and yolks. Pour about ½ cup of the hot mixture into the eggs and whisk well. Pour this back into the pan and, stirring constantly over low heat, cook until it registers 170°F on an instant-read thermometer. Do not boil. (If it does come to a boil, continue quickly to the next step.) Remove the pan from the heat, and stir in butter until well combined. Pour the pastry cream through a fine-mesh strainer into a clean bowl. Set the bowl in an ice bath to chill thoroughly. Place a piece of plastic wrap directly on the surface of the pastry cream to keep a skin from forming. When cool, whip pastry cream with 2 tablespoons sugar to firm peaks. Chill again. Best if used within 48 hours.

To make the no-cook filling, gently mix frozen whipped topping and condensed milk, then stir in lime juice and Kumquat Purée.

Preheat oven to 425°F and position a rack in the center of the oven. Line a sheet pan with parchment paper.

To make the dough, lightly flour work surface and roll the thawed pastry into a thin 16-inch square. Using a fork, prick the pastry all over, including the edges. Cut into 16 (3x3-inch) pieces. Place on prepared sheet pan and chill in the freezer, about 20 minutes. Bake until slightly puffed and browned, about 20 minutes. Cool on rack.

To assemble, place a pastry rectangle, shiny side up, on each dessert plate. Spread or pipe a layer of filling on top. Repeat layers and end with a fourth rectangle. Dust with confectioners' sugar and serve.

Kumquat, Oatmeal, and White Chocolate Cookies

Skip the raisins and go for the kumquats and white chocolate chips —
oatmeal cookies reimagined! Go on, be a bit daring!

Makes about 30

Preheat oven to 375°F and position a rack in the center of the oven.

Place butter and brown sugar in the bowl of a stand mixer fitted with the paddle attachment, and beat until fluffy. Add eggs and mix well. In a separate bowl, combine oats, flour, baking soda, and salt. Gradually add dry ingredients to butter mixture until fully combined. Stir in kumquat pieces and chips and place large teaspoonfuls onto ungreased sheet pans. Bake 10 to 15 minutes, or until golden brown. Place cookies on rack to cool. Store in an airtight container.

⅔ cup unsalted butter

⅔ cup light brown sugar

2 eggs

1½ cups old-fashioned rolled oats

2 cups unbleached all-purpose flour

1 teaspoon baking soda

1 teaspoon salt

⅔ cup chopped kumquat halves from Kumquat Conserve (page 14)

⅔ cup good quality white chocolate chips

Kumquat Palmiers

Mixed up in 15 minutes and baked in 15 more, these delicate pastries are a cinch to make. Only three ingredients, a little time, a pot of tea, and you're on your way to enjoying a nice afternoon break. Of course, it's up to you, but I prefer not to dunk. I love the crispiness of palmiers.

Makes 30 to 40

1¼ cups seeded and chopped fresh kumquats or kumquat halves from Kumquat Conserve (page 14)

1½ cups granulated sugar, divided

1 sheet frozen puff pastry, thawed and refrigerated until ready to use

Place fresh kumquats or halves from Kumquat Conserve in the bowl of a food processor and pulse until the mixture is smooth. Transfer to a small bowl and set aside.

Scatter ½ cup sugar, instead of flour, on your work surface to keep the dough from sticking. Place the thawed puff pastry on the work surface and scatter ½ cup sugar over the top. Roll out into a 12½x15-inch rectangle, embedding the sugar into the dough. Evenly spread the kumquat mixture on the pastry, stopping ½ inch from each side. Fold each long side about 1½ inches in toward the center. Repeat folding each side toward the center until the folded edges meet. Then where the edges meet, fold the dough in half one final time so that one folded side is atop the other. Cover in plastic wrap and chill until very firm, at least 1 hour.

Preheat oven to 400°F and position a rack in the center of the oven. Line ½-inch sided sheet pans with parchment paper.

When ready to bake, cut the dough into ¼-inch-thick slices. Place remaining ½ cup sugar on a plate. Coat cookies in sugar and arrange on prepared sheet pans at least 1 inch apart so they have room to expand. Bake for 10 minutes. Remove the pan from the oven and close the door. Using a spatula, quickly flip the cookies over and return the pan to the oven. Bake for another 5 minutes, or until cookies are a deep golden brown color. Place pan on a rack to cool. Repeat as needed. Store in sealed container.

ABOUT PALMIERS

A palmier is a crunchy type of sugar cookie. It is thought to have originated in France around the turn of the twentieth century, but it is also found in Italian, Spanish, Jewish, German, Chinese, and Portuguese cuisines. In French, *palmier* means palm leaf, but around the world, it has also been called an elephant ear, pig's ear, French heart, or glasses. Palmiers are made from puff pastry, a finely layered dough similar to croissant dough but without yeast. Usually palmiers are rolled in sugar before baking, and in Puerto Rico, they are topped with honey.

KUMQUAT, BLOOD ORANGE, AND CASHEW BISCOTTI

In the Kumquat Palmier recipe, I said "no dunking," but with biscotti, it's almost mandatory that you do. Ever try dipping your biscotti in wine? If you haven't, you might want to try these with a quick dip into a sweet white wine for dessert, but coffee and tea are great, too.

Makes 28 to 40, depending on cut

Preheat oven to 350°F and position a rack in the center of the oven. Line a half-sheet or jellyroll pan with parchment paper.

In the bowl of a stand mixer fitted with the paddle attachment, beat flour, sugar, baking soda, baking powder, and salt. Set aside. In a separate bowl, combine blood orange juice, honey, Kumquat Purée, and blood orange zest. Carefully add this to the mixer and blend just until the mixture looks shaggy and there are still patches of flour. Add the cashews and kumquat pieces, and continue mixing on low until the dough is cohesive and there are no more streaks of flour.

Divide the dough in half. On a lightly floured surface, roll each half into a log about 14 inches long. Transfer to the prepared pan and press slightly so that the width of each log is about 2 inches.

Bake for 30 minutes, or until golden brown and firm to the touch. Place pan on a rack to cool completely. Lower oven temperature to 250°F.

Cut the logs on a diagonal into ½-inch-thick cookies. Place the cookies cut side down on sheet pan. Bake for 15 minutes, flip the cookies and bake for an additional 15 minutes, or until the biscotti are lightly golden and very dry. Cool completely. Store in an airtight container.

- 2¼ cups unbleached all-purpose flour
- ½ cup granulated sugar
- ¾ teaspoon baking soda
- 1 teaspoon baking powder
- ¼ teaspoon salt
- ¼ cup blood orange juice
- ¼ cup orange blossom honey
- 2 tablespoons Kumquat Purée (page 14)
- 1 tablespoon grated blood orange zest
- 1 cup roasted, unsalted cashews
- ½ cup chopped kumquat halves from Kumquat Conserve (page 14)

KUMQUAT SCONES WITH
BLOOD ORANGE ZEST AND CANDIED GINGER

This is one of my favorite kumquat recipes. I make these luscious scones whenever we have overnight guests, and they are always met with rave reviews. I knew this recipe was a keeper when I won a Best of Division Award at the San Diego County Fair.
Put the kettle on! Time for scones and tea!

Makes 8

2 tablespoons granulated sugar

⅓ cup chopped candied or crystallized ginger

2½ cups unbleached all-purpose flour

¼ teaspoon salt

2 teaspoons baking powder

1 large blood orange, zested

½ cup (1 stick) cold unsalted butter, cut into pieces

1 cup chopped and rinsed kumquat halves from Kumquat Conserve (page 14)

¾ cup cold heavy cream

Finishing Touches

2 to 3 tablespoons heavy cream

Granulated sugar

Preheat oven to 425°F and position a rack in the center of the oven. Stack two 15x10-inch sheet pans on top of each other and line the top pan with parchment paper. (This double-panning will prevent the bottom of the scones from over browning.)

Place sugar and candied or crystallized ginger in the bowl of a food processor and process until ginger is very finely chopped. Add flour, salt, baking powder, blood orange zest, and butter pieces, and pulse until butter is the size of small peas.

Transfer mixture to a bowl and stir in kumquats. Add heavy cream and mix until just blended. Do not beat or the scones will be tough. Turn mixture out onto a lightly floured surface and knead two or three times, just to bring the dough together. Pat into a 7-inch circle, and use a large knife to cut the circle into eight equal wedges. (At this point the scones can be refrigerated overnight or frozen, well wrapped, for up to 1 month.)

To finish, place scones on the prepared sheet pan. Brush tops with 2 to 3 tablespoons heavy cream and sprinkle with sugar. Bake for 15 to 18 minutes, or until firm to the touch and golden brown. Place pan on rack to cool. Store in an airtight container.

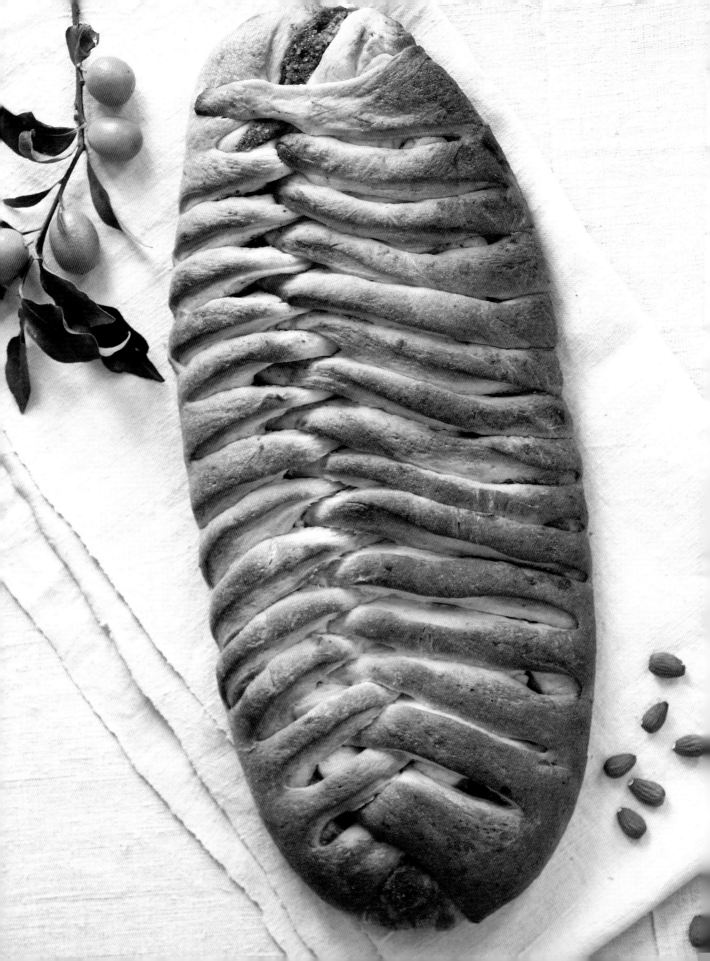

KUMQUAT ALMOND BREAKFAST BRAID

I love baking yeasted breads. There is something almost sacred in this process. I get a special satisfaction watching the dough rise, knowing that part of the fun is in the waiting and anticipation . . . the heavenly scent of warm bread will soon be filling my kitchen. But even more important, somewhere in my being I am connected to an age-old process that gives me a sense of peace and a feeling of kinship to all women throughout time who have baked bread in their homes to nurture their families.

Makes 1

Line a 12x18-inch half sheet pan with parchment paper or a silicone mat.

To make the dough, place warmed milk and sugar in the bowl of a stand mixer fitted with the paddle attachment. Whisk in yeast and allow the mixture to stand for about 5 minutes, or until the yeast is active and bubbling.

Add eggs and mix until well combined. Add flour and salt and mix on low to blend well. Switch to the dough hook and knead the dough for 2 minutes on medium speed. With the mixer running on medium, slowly add butter, about 2 tablespoons at a time, allowing each addition to become absorbed into the dough before adding the next. Once all the butter has been added, continue to knead the dough for 5 minutes, or until soft and silky.

Place dough in a lightly buttered or oiled bowl and cover with a towel or plastic wrap. Set in a warm place to rise until doubled in size, about 1 to 1½ hours. (This may take more or less time depending on the warmth of the room.)

To make the filling, place butter and sugar in the bowl of a stand mixer fitted with the paddle attachment. Beat on medium speed for 2 minutes, or until well blended and slightly lightened in color. Beat in almond liqueur or extract. Add ground almonds and beat well. Add kumquat pieces and beat just until blended. Set aside.

Remove dough from the bowl, place on a lightly floured surface, and dust the top with flour. Roll dough into a 12x17-inch rectangle, dusting the surface with flour as needed to keep dough from sticking. Turn dough so the short edge is parallel to you and the edge of your work surface. Brush any excess flour from the surface. Spread the filling down the center of the dough, about 3½ inches wide, stopping ½ inch before the bottom of dough. »

Dough

1 cup whole milk, warmed to lukewarm, about 90°F

½ cup granulated sugar

1 tablespoon active dry yeast

2 large eggs, room temperature

4 cups unbleached all-purpose flour

1 teaspoon salt

1 cup (2 sticks) unsalted butter, room temperature

Filling

½ cup (1 stick) unsalted butter, softened

¾ cup granulated sugar

2 tablespoons Amaretto di Saronno or other almond liqueur (or 2 teaspoons pure almond extract)

1¼ cups finely ground toasted almonds

1⅓ cups chopped kumquat halves from Kumquat Conserve (page 14)

<< Use a sharp knife to cut 14 to 16 downward-slanting lines on each side of the filling. Try to match the cuts on both sides for the best-looking braid. Assuming your dough is 12 inches wide and the filling about 3½ inches wide, your cuts will be approximately 3½ to 4 inches long and about ½ to ¾ inches wide. Fold the strips of pastry into the center, criss-crossing the filling by alternating one strip from the left side of the pastry with one from the right. Make the folds fairly tight, with no filling showing through, except at the top starting point. When you reach the end of the braid, press the ends into the dough and fold the bottom under to achieve a neat, finished look.

Carefully transfer the braid to the prepared sheet pan. Cover with a towel or loose plastic wrap and allow to rise in a warm place until fully risen and puffy, about 30 to 40 minutes.

Preheat oven to 400°F and position a rack in the center of the oven.

Bake for 20 to 25 minutes, or until golden brown. Place pan on rack to cool slightly. Serve warm or at room temperature.

Kumquat Noodle Pudding (Kugel)

Noodle pudding, also known as kugel, is a festive Eastern European Jewish dessert often served on holidays and special occasions. Kugels come in every variety imaginable and are relatively simple to make.

Serves 6 to 8

Preheat oven to 375°F and position a rack in the center of the oven. Grease a 2-quart baking dish.

In a bowl beat egg yolks. Stir in butter, sugar, salt, and your choice of seasoning. Add noodles, Kumquat Conserve, raisins, and walnuts. Mix again. In the bowl of a stand mixer fitted with the whisk attachment, beat egg whites until stiff but not dry, and fold into noodle mixture gently but thoroughly. Pour into prepared baking dish. Bake for 40 minutes, or until set and lightly browned on top.

4 eggs, separated

4 tablespoons melted butter

3 tablespoons granulated sugar

½ teaspoon salt

1 teaspoon cardamom, ginger, or almond extract, or ¼ teaspoon saffron

½ pound medium egg noodles, cooked and drained

1 cup Kumquat Conserve (page 14)

½ cup seedless raisins

¼ cup coarsely chopped walnuts

KUMQUAT RICE PUDDING

*Rice pudding is another one of those comfort foods that remind me of my childhood.
When one of us was under the weather, you can bet a big bubbling pot of
rice pudding would magically appear on the stove.*

Serves 6

2 cups water

1 cup medium- or short-grain white rice

2 teaspoons almond extract

1 (12-ounce) can evaporated milk

1 (14-ounce) can sweetened condensed milk

¾ cup Kumquat Conserve (page 14)

1½ teaspoons vanilla extract

¼ teaspoon salt

2 large eggs

Finishing Touch

Fresh mint leaves

Place water, rice, and almond extract in a large saucepan and bring to a boil. Reduce heat to low. Cover and cook 12 to 15 minutes, or until liquid is absorbed. Stir in evaporated milk, sweetened condensed milk, Kumquat Conserve, vanilla, and salt. Bring to a boil. Place eggs in a separate bowl and beat slightly. Stir a small portion of the rice mixture into the eggs to warm them. Add the eggs to the rice mixture and mix well with wire whisk. Bring to a boil. Cook, stirring constantly, for 2 minutes. Serve warm or chilled, garnished with mint leaves.

Coconut Tapioca Pudding with Kumquat Ginger Syrup

There's something about tapioca that's very soothing to me. I would definitely label it one of my comfort foods. My mom would make it for us in the winter, and if my sister and I were lucky, we'd get the wooden spoon and the almost-empty saucepan to lap up every last bit. I've always secretly wondered if my mom purposely didn't scrape the pan very well so there would be more for us. I'll have to ask my sister....

Serves 6

To make the pudding, bring 2 inches of water to a boil in the bottom of a double boiler. Place coconut milk, sugar, and split vanilla bean in the top portion of double boiler and set over the gently boiling water. When the mixture is hot, add the tapioca and cook, stirring frequently, for 45 to 55 minutes, or until the tapioca is completely cooked and translucent. Remove the tapioca from the heat and place a piece of plastic wrap directly on the surface of the pudding. Refrigerate until completely chilled, at least 3 hours, or place over an ice bath to cool more quickly.

To assemble the dessert, line up 6 champagne flutes or parfait glasses. Stir the tapioca pudding to break the "gel" and distribute any extra liquid. Discard the vanilla bean. Transfer the pudding to a pastry bag fitted with a ½-inch plain tip. Pipe about an inch of pudding in the bottom of each glass. Top with 1 teaspoon of the kumquat ginger syrup. Pipe another layer of pudding and top with another teaspoon of syrup. Continue layering until flutes or glasses are full.

5 cups canned full-fat (not "lite") coconut milk

½ cup granulated sugar

1 vanilla bean, split

½ cup small pearl tapioca

1¼ cups chilled Kumquat Ginger Syrup (page 14)

Kumquat Blood Orange Ginger Parfait

The word parfait literally means "perfect" in France, where the parfait originated. Originally a parfait was a layered ice cream dessert served in a fluted glass, but the American version evolved into combinations of pudding, custard, fruit, flavored gelatin, and ice cream, all topped off with whipped cream. My version showcases kumquat and blood orange fillings. Best to get a long-handled ice tea spoon and dig in!

Serves 6

Bottom Layer

¼ cup plus 6 tablespoons whole milk, divided

1¼ teaspoons powdered unflavored gelatin

¾ cup heavy cream

1 (3-inch piece) peeled ginger, roughly chopped

¼ cup granulated sugar

Middle Layer

1 cup strained blood orange juice, divided

1 teaspoon powdered unflavored gelatin

¼ cup Kumquat Ginger Syrup (page 14)

⅓ cup whole milk

1½ teaspoons granulated sugar

Top Layer

2 tablespoons plus ⅔ cup strained blood orange juice, divided

1 teaspoon powdered unflavored gelatin

6 tablespoons Kumquat Ginger Syrup (page 14)

1 tablespoon granulated sugar, or to taste

Finishing Touch

Lightly sweetened whipped cream

To prepare the bottom layer, pour ¼ cup milk in a small bowl, sprinkle gelatin over the top, and gently stir to make sure all granules are moistened. Set aside for 5 minutes.

Pour the remaining 6 tablespoons of milk into a medium saucepan. Add cream, ginger, and sugar. Heat just until it begins to simmer. Remove from the heat, cover the pan, and let steep for 30 minutes. Pour through a fine-mesh strainer, pressing against the solids to remove as much liquid as possible. Discard the solids.

Bring 2 inches of water to a simmer in a large sauté pan. Turn off the heat and place the bowl with the milk and gelatin into the hot water bath. Stir gently until the gelatin completely melts and the milk looks smooth. Add this to the cream mixture and stir until well blended. Divide the mixture evenly among the glasses. Refrigerate until the bottom layer is set, at least 1½ hours.

For the middle layer, place 2 tablespoons of blood orange juice in a small bowl. Sprinkle gelatin over the top and gently stir to make sure all granules are moistened. Set aside for 5 minutes.

In a bowl, combine remaining blood orange juice, Kumquat Ginger Syrup, milk, and sugar. Stir gently until sugar dissolves. Bring 2 inches of water to a simmer in a large sauté pan. Turn off the heat and place the bowl with the gelatin and blood orange juice into the hot water bath. Stir gently until the gelatin completely melts and the blood orange juice looks smooth. Add this to the blood orange ginger mixture and stir until well blended. Remove the glasses from the refrigerator and divide the mixture evenly among them. Return them to the refrigerator until the middle layer is set, at least 1½ hours. ››

≪ To make the top layer, place 2 tablespoons blood orange juice in a small bowl. Sprinkle the gelatin over the top and gently stir to make sure all granules are moistened. Set aside for 5 minutes.

In a medium bowl, combine the ⅔ cup blood orange juice, Kumquat Ginger Syrup, and sugar to taste. Stir gently until the sugar dissolves. Bring 2 inches of water to a simmer in a large sauté pan. Turn off the heat and place the bowl with the gelatin and blood orange juice into the hot water bath. Stir gently until the gelatin completely melts and the blood orange juice looks smooth. Add this to the blood orange mixture and stir until well blended. Remove the glasses from the refrigerator and divide the mixture evenly among them. Return them to the refrigerator until the top layer is set, at least 1 hour.

To serve, garnish with a spoonful of lightly sweetened whipped cream. Serve parfaits cold with chilled iced tea spoons.

GREEK YOGURT PANNA COTTA WITH HONEYED KUMQUAT SAUCE

I think Italian cooks got it right when they mixed cream and sugar with gelatin to create panna cotta. I just love the creamy quasi-solid texture. I added Greek yogurt to this recipe to punch up the tang factor and found it to be a nice balance with the kumquats and honey. You can also toss on a few walnuts before serving and make it even more Greek.

Serves 6

Panna Cotta

2 tablespoons cold water

1¼ teaspoons powdered unflavored gelatin

2 cups heavy cream

⅓ cup sugar

1½ cups plain Greek yogurt

Kumquat Sauce

½ cup Kumquat Purée (page 14)

½ cup water, or more as needed to thin

½ cup honey

Finishing Touches

Kumquat halves from Kumquat Conserve (page 14)

Lightly coat 6 (8-ounce) custard cups or ramekins with a flavorless vegetable oil (such as canola oil) spray.

To make the panna cotta, place water in a small bowl and sprinkle gelatin over the top. Set aside to allow the gelatin to soften for 5 minutes.

In a saucepan, heat heavy cream and sugar over medium heat, just until the mixture is hot and the sugar dissolves. Do not boil. Turn off the heat, whisk in yogurt, and add the gelatin mixture. Stir until the gelatin dissolves and blends completely with the cream mixture. Pour through a fine-mesh strainer into a large measuring cup or container. Divide the mixture among the prepared cups (about ½ cup in each). Cover each with plastic wrap and refrigerate. Chill until firm, about 2 to 3 hours. The panna cotta may be prepared a day in advance.

To make the kumquat sauce, place Kumquat Purée, water, honey, in a medium saucepan over medium heat. Bring to a boil, then lower the heat and simmer for about 5 minutes, or just until slightly thickened. Remove from the heat and stir in the kumquat halves from the conserve. Cool completely before using. Place in an ice bath to quickly chill, if desired.

To assemble, run a thin knife or small spatula around the edges of each ramekin, being careful not to gouge the sides of the cream as you do this. Dip each cup in hot water for 2 to 3 seconds to help the cream loosen and slide from the cup. Wipe the cup dry, then invert onto a plate. If the custard does not slide out, grab the plate and cup together and shake them gently, forcing the cream to plop out. Spoon some of the cold honeyed kumquat sauce over and around each panna cotta. Serve immediately. Garnish with kumquat halves.

TROPICAL KUMQUAT SORBET

Serve this as a perfect refresher between courses or enjoy a bowlful while sitting outside on a summer night listening to the cicadas and searching for Venus.

Makes about 1 quart

Note: *If you have a frozen canister-style ice cream machine, allow 24 hours for the canister to freeze.*

Combine all ingredients in a medium bowl and whisk to blend thoroughly. Taste and adjust the flavors to your liking. Freeze in an ice cream machine according to manufacturer's directions. When the sorbet is done, spoon into bowls and drizzle with Kumquat Conserve or transfer to an airtight storage container and place in the freezer until ready to serve.

1 cup plus 2 tablespoons Kumquat Ginger Syrup (page 14)

½ cup unsweetened pineapple juice

1 (14-ounce) can full-fat (not "lite") coconut milk

1 teaspoon strained blood orange juice

Finishing Touch
Kumquat Conserve (page 14)

Kumquat Ginger Ice Cream

All hail ice cream, my most indulgent pleasure! I like to make it myself because I know the purity of the ingredients, and furthermore, I've never seen this flavor served anywhere except from my kitchen. And although half a cup is a serving, you just might want a smidge more. If you are feeling particularly indulgent, top it off with a spoonful of buttery caramel sauce or a splash of dark bittersweet chocolate sauce.

Makes about 1½ quarts

1½ cups whole milk

1½ cups heavy cream

½ cup sugar

4 large egg yolks

1 cup chilled Kumquat
Ginger Syrup (page 14)

1¼ cups chopped kumquat
halves from Kumquat
Conserve (page 14)

Note: *If you have a frozen canister-style ice cream machine, allow 24 hours for the canister to freeze.*

Warm milk and cream in a medium saucepan over medium-low heat to just below the boiling point. In a small bowl, whisk together sugar and egg yolks. Whisking the yolks constantly, slowly add about 1 cup of the hot cream to the yolks. Pour the yolk mixture back into the saucepan and cook, stirring constantly with a wooden spoon, until the custard thickens slightly and coats the back of the spoon (about 170°F on an instant-read thermometer). Immediately pour the custard through a fine-mesh strainer into a large bowl. Set the bowl in an ice bath and stir the custard until it is cold. Stir in Kumquat Ginger Syrup.

Freeze in an ice cream machine according to manufacturer's directions. When the ice cream is done, transfer it to an airtight storage container and stir in kumquat pieces. Cover and place in the freezer until ready to serve.

BLOOD ORANGES

The Beauty of the Blood Orange

An excerpt from "One Ingredient: Many Ways"
by Leah Koenig, originally published on Saveur.com

"A friend once said to me, 'If you ever want to confirm the existence of miracles, just look at a sliced red onion.' I immediately fell for the idea that, when paid the proper attention, a fruit or vegetable could be so extraordinary — so arresting in its beauty — that it evokes a sense of the sacred. After that, I started noticing 'miracle produce' everywhere, from Romanesco cauliflower with its fractal-shaped florets, to the thin fuchsia rings of a chioggia beet, and, most recently, blood oranges. Outside, a blood orange looks like any other thick-skinned navel, with just the slightest blush indicating that something special might be hiding inside. But slice it open, and the shock of glistening, sunset-stained flesh feels nothing short of miraculous."

Blood Orange:
The Ruby of the Orange Family

WITH ITS DISTINCTIVE COLOR AND COMPLEX flavor, the blood orange is the crown jewel of the orange family. It is generally smaller than the average orange, and its taste is hard to describe — some say it has berry or raspberry undertones, others a grape-like flavor, but I believe it has a slightly floral note. I just really can't compare it to anything else. A blood orange tastes like an orange with a kick.

The beautiful flesh of the blood orange varies in color from a few reddish streaks to a very dark maroon, almost purple-black. Various shades of red can also appear on the rind. The flesh gets its color from anthocyanins, which are red-pigmented antioxidants occurring in vegetables, flowers, and fruit, but not in citrus except for the blood orange. When it grows in hot, sunny days and cold nights, the flesh darkens, developing its characteristic color because the "ruby" gene, as it is called, becomes more expressed. Since they need these extremes in temperature, blood oranges are cultivated primarily in California and Texas, and in Europe around Sicily, Italy, as well as Spain and North Africa. In the United States, blood oranges are in season from January to June.

A number of stories exist about how this delightful fruit came into being. The first mention of "red oranges" appeared in the seventeenth and eighteenth centuries when a Jesuit priest wrote that a missionary traveling from Asia introduced blood oranges to Italy. Also about that time, blood oranges began showing up in paintings and botanical drawings. The blood orange is believed to have originated in China or the southern Mediterranean region and was introduced to the U.S. in the 1930s by Spanish and Italian immigrants.

There are three common varieties of the blood orange, which scientists agree is a natural mutation of the sweet orange, also known as the blonde orange. Moros are the darkest blood oranges, with flesh so dark they can appear almost black. They have a flavor much stronger and an aroma more intense than a normal orange with few or no seeds. The Sanguinello from Spain has a medium orange color, reddish skin, and a sweet and tender flesh. The Tarocco, the most popular variety in Italy, is considered the sweetest of the blood oranges, is also seedless and easy to peel. At Beck Grove, we grow Moros and Taroccos.

Italians prize blood oranges much more than Americans do, and Sicilians, who are especially fond of their local harvest, serve blood oranges at the end of the meal or in a simple salad with red onions, fresh fennel, olive oil, and salt and pepper. In restaurants, blood oranges are most often used in desserts. When squeezed, their juice is a beautiful color, creating a most unusual fresh citrus drink. Fantastic as a juice mixer or eaten right off the tree, the blood orange complements seafood and other entrées. The blood orange's delicate white flower is also memorable for its creamy tropical fragrance. Blood oranges are very nutritious too, packing a large punch of Vitamin C, fiber, and antioxidants. They will keep at room temperature for several days in an open bowl or basket.

BLOOD ORANGE SALAD WITH CANDIED ALMONDS

Candied almonds make this salad a special treat. There are many uses for the blood orange infusion — try it as a marinade; drizzle it over lightly steamed vegetables; baste fish, pork, or poultry before roasting; use it as a base for a citrus vinaigrette, or as a simple dressing as I do here. Beware of the candied almonds, they are addicting!

Serves 4

To make the infusion, place the olive oil in a bowl. Cut the skin off the blood oranges and squeeze the juice and the skin into the olive oil. Discard the pulp, but place the skins into the oil as well. Squeezing the skin helps to release the oils inside the skin. Set aside. This step can be done up to a day ahead.

To make the candied almonds, preheat oven to 300°F and line a sheet pan with parchment paper.

In a small bowl, combine both sugars, salt, and ginger or spicy seasoning, if desired. Make sure there are no lumps. Set aside. In another small bowl, beat egg white and water until frothy but not stiff. Coat almonds in the egg white and then in the sugar mixture. Spread in a single layer on the prepared sheet pan. Bake for 30 minutes, stirring occasionally. Place pan on a rack to cool, making sure to separate any nuts that stick together.

In a large bowl, gently combine mache, jicama, and endive. Plate the greens, top with orange rounds, and liberally drizzle with infused olive oil. Garnish with candied almonds, kumquat slices, and fresh chopped parsley.

Serve with a side dish of crème fraîche, if desired.

Blood Orange Infusion
- ½ cup extra virgin olive oil
- 2 blood oranges

Candied Almonds
- ¼ cup dark brown sugar
- ½ cup granulated sugar
- 1 to 1½ teaspoons salt
- ½ teaspoon ground ginger
- 1 teaspoon, cayenne, smoked paprika, or your favorite spicy or hot seasoning, if desired
- 1 egg white, room temperature
- 1 tablespoon water
- 1 pound whole almonds

Greens
- 4 cups loosely packed mache or other tender leaf lettuce
- ½ cup julienned jicama
- 2 or 3 endives, cut in ¾-inch sections
- 2 blood oranges, peeled and sliced into rounds

Finishing Touches
- ½ cup thinly sliced and seeded fresh kumquats
- ¼ cup crème fraîche, if desired
- Chopped fresh Italian parsley, if desired

BLOOD ORANGE SPINACH SALAD

This delightful tart and sweet citrus dressing is one you'll want to keep on hand for a variety of salads. It's particularly good on this very simple spinach salad. To turn it into an entrée, crumble feta cheese on top or add sliced chicken or turkey breast.

Serves 2

Dressing

2 tablespoons blood orange juice

2 tablespoons white wine vinegar

3 tablespoons extra virgin olive oil

2 teaspoons honey

1 tablespoon chopped fresh cilantro leaves

2 teaspoons Dijon mustard

Salt and freshly ground black pepper, to taste

Greens

2 cups fresh spinach or your favorite lettuce

½ small red onion, thinly sliced

2 blood oranges, peeled and segmented

4 tablespoons raw or toasted pine nuts

In a small bowl, whisk together dressing ingredients. Plate the greens and garnish with red onion, orange segments, and pine nuts. Drizzle with dressing and serve.

ABOUT PINE NUTS

Ever wonder if pine nuts are really from pine trees? They are, but they are actually the seeds, not nuts, that mature within the pine cone. Pine nuts have been used as food in Europe and Asia since the Paleolithic period, as long as 2.6 million years ago! Today, they are used throughout Europe, the Middle East, Asia, and North America, and are the essential component of a number of dishes, including pesto and pine nut cookies that are popular in Italy.

Grilled Sirloin with Blood Oranges, Asiago, and Greens

Grill a sirloin and do something different — serve it with blood oranges and shards of Asiago cheese over tender greens. If you want to make the meal extra special, pile Parmesan cheese into little mounds on a parchment-lined sheet pan and toast under the broiler until crispy. To make the dish even more flavorful, double the vinaigrette recipe and marinate the beef for 4 hours or overnight in the refrigerator before grilling.

Serves 4 to 6

To make the vinaigrette, combine first 5 ingredients in a bowl and whisk in oil until well blended. Before using, remove the smashed garlic clove.

To prepare the salad, toss greens, onion, and cucumber in a bowl with about half of the dressing. Plate the greens and top with steak and orange rounds. Drizzle with additional dressing, if desired. Garnish with Asiago cheese and season to taste.

Blood Orange Vinaigrette

- ½ cup blood orange juice (from 1 to 2 oranges)
- ¼ cup rice vinegar
- 1 small shallot, minced
- 1 clove garlic, smashed
- ⅛ teaspoon salt
- ½ cup extra virgin olive oil

Greens

- 6 cups green-leaf and red-leaf lettuces
- ¼ cup thinly sliced red onion
- 1 cup thinly sliced cucumber

Finishing Touches

- 1 pound grilled boneless beef sirloin, thinly sliced
- 2 blood oranges, peeled and sliced into rounds
- 2 ounces Asiago cheese, cut into shards
- Salt and freshly ground black pepper, to taste

Blood Orange Tuna-Stuffed Cherry Pepper Salad

When we were traveling in Italy, I was introduced to tuna-stuffed cherry peppers, and I fell in love with them! They are frequently served in Cichetti bars. Cichetti are to Italy what tapas are to Spain — small, bite-sized portions of food, typically eaten in one or two bites and nearly always enjoyed with a small glass of wine. I paired these with blood oranges and a blood orange vinaigrette and found the taste sublime.

Serves 4

Dressing

- **2 tablespoons blood orange juice**
- **1 tablespoon white wine vinegar**
- **4 tablespoons extra virgin olive oil**
- **2 teaspoons honey**
- **2 teaspoons Dijon mustard**
- **Salt and freshly ground black pepper, to taste**

Greens

- **4 cups fresh spinach leaves or torn Romaine lettuce**
- **½ small red onion, thinly sliced**
- **2 blood oranges, peeled and segmented**
- **16 dry-cured black olives**
- **8 to 12 tuna-stuffed cherry peppers (available online or at specialty stores)**

Whisk together all dressing ingredients. Season with salt and freshly ground black pepper. In a large bowl, gently combine spinach, red onion, orange segments, and black olives. Plate and lightly dress greens and top with stuffed cherry peppers.

CARAMELIZED BLOOD ORANGE PORK TENDERLOIN

This recipe works as well for chicken or duck as it does for pork. If using poultry, select skinless breasts or thighs and adjust the cooking time so the meat registers 165°F on an instant-read thermometer. Serve with jasmine rice or cook the rice in chicken stock and the liquid from the blood orange infusion.

Serves 6

To make the blood orange infusion, cut blood oranges in half and place in a large saucepan with kaffir leaves, lemongrass, olive oil, wine, and salt. Add water to completely cover blood oranges. Bring to a boil. Reduce heat and simmer until orange peels are tender, about 25 minutes. Remove from heat and cool. Drain and reserve the blood orange liquid for cooking the pork and rice, if desired. Carefully remove the blood orange peel from the flesh. Scrape off all white pith on the peels, leaving only the orange zest. Cut zest into 1-inch-wide strips.

Put the zest strips in a small container and completely cover with olive oil. Keep tightly sealed in the refrigerator until ready to use. Leftover zest will keep refrigerated for at least a week.

To prepare the meat, place pork on a clean work surface. Remove strips of zest from the oil, cut into ½-inch pieces, and layer over the pork. Sprinkle with ginger and salt, then firmly pat brown sugar on top.

To cook the pork, preheat oil from blood orange infusion in a skillet over medium heat. Place tenderloins sugar side down in the skillet. Cook without turning or moving for approximately 5 minutes. If the sugar begins to burn, reduce heat slightly. When the sugar side is well browned and caramelized, turn and sear remaining sides for 10 to 15 minutes more. Cook until meat registers an internal temperature of 145°F for medium rare or 150°F for medium on an instant-read thermometer.

Transfer to a carving board and allow to rest, tented loosely with foil, for 10 minutes before slicing. Season to taste with remaining salt and serve with blood orange slices and infused rice, if desired.

Blood Orange Infusion

4 blood oranges

2 fresh or dried kaffir lime leaves

2 (4-inch) stalks fresh lemongrass

3 tablespoons extra virgin olive oil

¾ cup dry white wine

2 teaspoons coarse salt

Extra virgin olive oil, to cover blood orange peel

Pork Tenderloin

1 to 2 pork tenderloins (about 2 pounds total)

Blood orange infusion zest strips

1 teaspoon grated fresh ginger

1 tablespoon coarse salt, or to taste

3 tablespoons light brown sugar

2 tablespoons blood orange infusion oil, for searing

Finishing Touches

Coarse salt, to taste

Blood orange slices

SOUTHWESTERN CHILI
WITH BLOOD ORANGE SAUCE

When I was developing this recipe, I wanted to add an ingredient that would complement the blood orange juice. So I gave dark rum a try. At first my husband was skeptical: "Rum in chili?" But it was perfect! For those of you who enjoy more spice, feel free to experiment with chili powder, cumin, or cayenne pepper.

Serves 6

3 to 4 pounds chicken pieces or 2 pounds boneless and skinless breasts

6 tablespoons extra virgin olive oil

3 onions, thinly sliced

6 cloves garlic, minced

4½ cups blood orange juice (from about 8 oranges)

1½ cups chicken broth

1 tablespoon prepared chili sauce

3 (15-ounce) cans black beans, rinsed and drained

1 cup fresh or frozen corn

3 tablespoons dark rum

Salt, to taste

Finishing Touches

1 pound cooked and drained pasta

Fresh minced cilantro leaves

2 blood oranges, peeled and segmented

To prepare the chicken, skin and debone white and dark meat or use boneless and skinless breasts. Chop meat into roughly 1-inch pieces. Heat oil in a large, deep skillet and brown chicken on all sides. Transfer to paper towels to drain.

In the same skillet, cook onion and garlic until tender. Return browned chicken to skillet and add blood orange juice, chicken broth, and chili sauce. Bring to a boil, reduce heat, and simmer over low heat for 30 minutes. Stir in black beans, corn, and rum. Cover and simmer for 10 more minutes, or until chicken is done.

Transfer chicken to a serving dish along with your favorite cooked pasta. One of my favorite pasta shapes is radiatore.

Simmer sauce, uncovered, for 5 minutes more, until slightly thickened. Season with salt to taste. Spoon sauce over chicken and garnish with fresh cilantro and blood orange segments.

TUNISIAN CHICKEN WINGS WITH BLOOD ORANGES

Americans are familiar with hot wings or buffalo wings that are bathed in a cayenne butter hot sauce and fried. My version features homemade harissa, a traditional North African seasoning paste made from hot peppers, olive oil, and aromatics. I prefer a combination of California and ancho chiles with their mild-to-medium heat, but use whatever dried chiles you like. Don't limit yourself to just these wings with harissa — try it on grilled meats, vegetables, rice, or pasta.

Serves 4

To make the harissa, soak the dried chiles in hot water for 30 minutes. Drain. Remove stems and seeds. In a food processor, combine peppers, garlic, salt, and 2 tablespoons olive oil. Pulse until smooth. Add spices and pulse until smooth. Transfer to a glass container, top with remaining olive oil, cover tightly, and refrigerate. Harissa will keep for at least a month refrigerated.

Preheat broiler or a grill to high.

To make the wing sauce, mix harissa, olive oil, and salt in a small bowl to make a paste. Brush wings with harissa mixture and coat well. Grill or broil for 5 to 8 minutes per side, until a dark golden brown.

While the wings are cooking, dip the blood orange quarters in the superfine sugar and grill or broil for a few minutes, until they are slightly burnt but not black or charred.

Serve wings and blood orange pieces immediately. Garnish with cilantro, if desired.

Harissa

10 to 12 dried red chile peppers

3 cloves garlic, minced

½ teaspoon salt

4 tablespoons olive oil, divided

1 teaspoon freshly ground coriander

1 teaspoon freshly ground caraway seeds

1 teaspoon freshly ground cumin

Wing Sauce

4 tablespoons harissa

2 tablespoons extra virgin olive oil

⅛ teaspoon salt

16 to 20 chicken wings

Finishing Touch

4 blood oranges, quartered

⅓ cup superfine sugar

ABOUT HARISSA

Harissa is a hot chili sauce or paste common in North Africa and often made from bird's-eye (*piri piri*) chiles or other hot peppers, spices, herbs, and vegetable or olive oil. The most commonly used aromatics are garlic, coriander, red chili powder, and caraway seeds. Harissa is frequently used in meat or fish stews, as a rub or marinade for meat or eggplant, and in chickpea soup and couscous. Look for it in a jar or can in Middle Eastern or specialty markets or your local grocery store, if you're lucky.

LOBSTER CORN CAKES WITH BLOOD ORANGES AND AVOCADOS

These are always a favorite. They are crunchy on the outside and tender and sweet inside. When I think of summertime in New England, I think of grilling lobster and corn on the beach with good friends and ice-cold beer. These lobster corn cakes bring that scene to mind. Serve them for Sunday brunch, a luncheon, or a light supper. If you make the corn cakes silver dollar size, they also make great hors d'oeuvres for cocktail parties.

Makes 6 to 8

⅓ cup whole milk

2 eggs

¼ teaspoon dried oregano

½ teaspoon dried cumin

¾ cup cornmeal

¼ cup unbleached all-purpose flour

2 small cooked lobsters, meat diced

1½ cups fresh corn kernels (from about 3 ears)

3 green onions, minced

1 yellow bell pepper, seeded and minced

1 small jalapeño pepper, seeded and minced

2 tablespoons vegetable oil, for oiling griddle or skillet

Finishing Touches

6 tablespoons extra virgin olive oil

2 tablespoons rice vinegar

⅛ teaspoon cayenne pepper

Salt, to taste

½ pound mixed greens

2 blood oranges, peeled and segmented

1 or 2 avocados, sliced

To make the batter, combine milk, eggs, oregano, cumin, cornmeal, and flour in a bowl until well blended. In a separate bowl, mix lobster, corn, onions, and both peppers. Gently combine lobster and flour mixtures and refrigerate for 5 to 10 minutes.

To cook the cakes, preheat a lightly oiled griddle or skillet to medium. For each cake, spread ½ cup batter into roughly a 3-inch circle and cook until the edges dry. Flip, and continue cooking until golden brown. Transfer to a serving plate and keep warm.

In a bowl, combine olive oil, rice vinegar, cayenne pepper, and salt. Gently toss in mixed greens, blood orange segments, and avocado slices.

To serve, plate lobster corn cakes and top with a handful of greens.

CRAB CAKES WITH
BLOOD ORANGES AND PAPAYA SAUCE

Crab cakes originated in the Chesapeake Bay area of Maryland, thanks to the abundance of blue crabs in the bay, but any crabmeat is good in this recipe. The papaya mayonnaise lends a tropical note and pretty hue to this dish. You can make them smaller and serve them as hors d'oeuvres. Prepare cakes the day before serving to let flavors develop.

Serves 6 (2 cakes per person)

Line sheet pans with parchment paper. Set aside.

To prepare the crab cakes, gently combine crabmeat, bell pepper, and jalapeño in a large bowl. Add thyme, mustard, sugar, eggs, mayonnaise, and ½ cup bread crumbs, and mix well. Form 12 small cakes, place on prepared pans, cover with plastic wrap, and refrigerate overnight.

To make the sauce, pulse the papaya chunks and lime juice in a food processor until smooth. Transfer to a bowl and stir in sugar and mayonnaise until well combined. Refrigerate until ready to serve.

To cook the crab cakes, place remaining bread crumbs in a shallow dish. Lightly coat chilled patties in crumbs. Heat butter in a large nonstick frying pan until hot. Gently lay crab cakes in the pan and fry 3 minutes per side, or until golden brown. Transfer to paper towels to drain.

To serve, plate crab cakes and garnish with blood orange segments, diced papaya, and a dollop of papaya sauce.

1 pound (about 2 cups) cooked crabmeat

1 red bell pepper, seeded and minced

1 jalapeño pepper, seeded and minced

1 teaspoon fresh thyme leaves

½ teaspoon dry mustard

1 teaspoon granulated sugar

2 large eggs

2 tablespoons good-quality mayonnaise

2½ cups unseasoned bread crumbs, divided

4 tablespoons unsalted butter, for frying

Sauce

1 cup papaya, peeled and chopped

1 lime, juiced

1 teaspoon granulated sugar, or to taste

2 tablespoons good-quality mayonnaise

Finishing Touches

Blood orange segments from 3 or 4 oranges

1 cup papaya, peeled and diced

MAHI-MAHI WITH BLOOD ORANGE SALSA

Marinating in lime juice, coconut milk, and ginger imparts a Thai flavor to the fish. Blood oranges team up with avocado for the salsa. I've also used this salsa as a condiment with tacos and burritos. This recipe can easily be doubled.

Serves 2

Marinade

2 limes, juiced

4 tablespoons full-fat (not "Lite") coconut milk

1 tablespoon peeled and minced fresh ginger

2 (6-ounce) fresh mahi-mahi fillets

Salt, to taste

Olive oil, for cooking

Salsa

2 blood oranges, peeled and segmented

½ cup avocado, diced

½ cup red bell pepper, diced

1 tablespoon chopped fresh cilantro leaves

2 tablespoons fresh Meyer lemon juice

Salt, to taste

To make the marinade, whisk together lime juice, coconut milk, and fresh ginger in a shallow glass or ceramic dish. Season mahi-mahi fillets with salt and place in the marinade. Cover and refrigerate for 20 to 30 minutes.

To make the salsa, gently combine blood orange segments, avocado, red bell pepper, cilantro, and lemon juice. Season with salt.

To cook the fish, heat a grill pan or skillet over medium heat. Drizzle with a small amount of olive oil. Cook fillets for 4 to 5 minutes on each side, or until the fish flakes easily with a fork.

To serve, plate fillets and spoon salsa over the top.

MOROCCAN FISH WITH BLOOD ORANGES

I've always been a fan of Moroccan cooking because of its complex blend of aromatics. One of the most amazing experiences of my life was wandering through the markets in Marrakech, where vendors proudly displayed piles of exotic herbs and colorful spices. I was entranced by the sights and smells all around me — cinnamon, turmeric, cumin, coriander, nutmeg, cloves, cardamom pods, saffron threads, and so many more. What an aromatic adventure!

Serves 4

Preheat oven to 425°F.

Place fish fillets in a baking dish and gently rub with *Ras el hanout*, making sure to coat them evenly.

In a bowl, whisk together blood orange juice and olive oil and pour over the fish. Sprinkle with olives. Bake until the fish is opaque and flakes easily with a fork, about 10 to 15 minutes.

Plate the fillets and black olives and garnish with blood orange segments. Delicious served with lightly sautéed greens.

4 (6-ounce) fresh cod fillets or your favorite fish

1½ tablespoons homemade or store-bought *Ras el hanout* (available online or at specialty stores)

2 blood oranges, juiced

3 tablespoons extra virgin olive oil

⅓ cup pitted black olives

Finishing Touch

Blood orange segments

ABOUT *RAS EL HANOUT*

Ras el hanout is a popular blend of Moroccan spices. The name translates as "head of the shop" in Arabic, meaning the mixture of the very best spices the merchant has to offer. The blend will vary from one person to the next, but it typically includes many of the traditional North African spices such as cumin, cloves, cardamom, cinnamon, coriander, turmeric, nutmeg, and various peppers. Some very exotic blends can contain up to 100 herbs and spices, including some rarely found in Western food. Typically the ingredients are roasted and ground together. If you want to make your own *Ras el hanout*, there are numerous recipes on the Internet that you can use as a base for your own unique blend.

BLOOD ORANGE CREPES

I favor these as dessert crepes, but they are also perfect for brunch. When strawberries or raspberries are in season, they are especially luscious, but you can use frozen berries, too. Like most crepes, they do take some time to make because of the various steps, but they are always compliment-worthy. You will get any where from 12 to 18 crepes. Fast on the pour and voila! Eighteen! My mother always prided herself that she could make 18 per batch of batter.

Makes 12 to 18, depending upon your skill as a crepemaker

Macerated Blood Oranges

1 cup blood orange segments

⅓ cup granulated sugar

Filling

1 cup cream cheese, softened

⅓ cup confectioners' sugar

1 cup sour cream

1 tablespoon fresh lemon juice

½ teaspoon blood orange zest

Sauce

¾ cup granulated sugar

½ cup water, divided

5 blood oranges, juiced with pulp

¼ teaspoon ground cardamom

¼ cup (½ stick) unsalted butter, cut into pieces

Batter

1 cup unbleached all-purpose flour

⅓ cup confectioners' sugar

¼ teaspoon salt

2 eggs

1½ cups whole milk

1 teaspoon blood orange zest

Unsalted butter, for cooking crepes

Finishing Touches

Fresh berries, if desired

Toasted pistachios, if desired

Place the blood orange segments in a bowl and coat them well with the sugar. Cover and refrigerate 1 hour.

To make the filling, beat the softened cream cheese and confectioners' sugar in the bowl of a stand mixer fitted with the paddle attachment until well blended. Add sour cream, lemon juice, and blood orange zest, and beat until smooth. Set aside.

To make the sauce, in a heavy saucepan, combine sugar and 2 tablespoons of water, and cook over moderately high heat, undisturbed, until sugar melts and syrup is golden. Remove pan from heat. Carefully drip remaining water down the side of the pan and stir in blood orange juice with pulp and cardamom. Be careful — the caramel will bubble up and steam. Return pan to heat and simmer, stirring, until caramel dissolves, about 5 minutes. Add butter, a piece at time, stirring until sauce is smooth. Sauce may be made 2 days ahead and chilled. Reheat sauce over low heat before serving.

To make the crepes, sift together dry ingredients. In a large bowl, beat eggs. Stir in milk, dry ingredients, and zest until well combined and smooth. Melt a little butter in 6-inch skillet or a crepe pan and add 3 tablespoons batter. Tip skillet from side to side until batter covers the bottom. Cook for about 30 seconds and flip. Repeat with the remaining batter. Crepes should be lightly browned on both sides. While cooking, stack crepes with a piece of parchment or wax paper between each one so they do not stick to each other.

To assemble, spread cream cheese filling evenly on crepe. Top with macerated blood oranges. Roll and place on plates. Pour sauce over crepes and garnish with fresh berries and pistachios, if desired. Serve immediately.

BLOOD ORANGE LADYFINGER TRIFLE

Elegant and brightly colorful, trifles always bring smiles and ooohs and ahhhs. Although the instructions appear lengthy, they are extremely easy. You are making a cooked custard to layer with blood oranges and ladyfingers soaked in a simple orange syrup. In the cold winter months when blood oranges are in season, this makes a very cheery dessert.

Serves 18 to 24, using an 8-inch trifle bowl (about 3 to 4 quarts)

To make the custard layer, fill the lower pan of a double boiler one-third full of water and bring to a low boil. Pour milk into the top pan and heat just until small bubbles form around the edges of the milk. Stir in sugar until it completely dissolves.

In a small bowl, beat the eggs until light yellow. Remove about ½ cup hot milk and gradually stir it into the eggs, then stir the mixture back into the milk in the top of the double boiler.

In a small bowl, combine cornstarch and water, then gently whisk it into the custard, stirring continuously until the custard thickens. It should stick to the back of a wooden spoon without dripping. Remove from heat. Stir in vanilla. Place a piece of plastic wrap directly on the surface of custard to keep a skin from forming. Chill thoroughly.

To prepare the blood oranges, cut off the ends of each blood orange and reserve the ends for juice and a little zest. Slice each blood orange into rounds and trim off the peel and white pith. Remove any seeds. Set aside. Zest one of the orange ends and julienne the zest into very thin strips to use as a garnish. Set aside. Squeeze the juice from the reserved ends of the oranges, and if needed, the juice from another round or two. This juice will be added to the blood orange syrup.

To make the blood orange syrup, combine all the syrup ingredients in a small saucepan and bring to a boil. Cook until syrupy, about 3 to 5 minutes. Remove rosemary. Cool to room temperature.

To make the whipped cream, beat heavy cream and sugar in the bowl of a stand mixer fitted with a whisk.

To assemble the trifle, you may follow the design of the trifle pictured or you can simply layer ingredients. Begin first by dipping ladyfingers in the blood orange syrup and covering the bottom of the footed dish. Then arrange and layer custard, blood orange rounds, whipped cream, pistachios, and more ladyfingers dipped in blood orange syrup. Repeat as necessary to fill the trifle bowl. Top with a dollop of whipped cream, pistachios, and julienned zest. Cover with plastic wrap and chill 2 hours before serving.

Custard

2 cups whole milk

¼ cup granulated sugar

2 eggs

1 tablespoon cornstarch

2 tablespoons water

1 teaspoon pure vanilla extract

Blood Oranges

8 to 10 blood oranges

Blood Orange Syrup

½ cup granulated sugar

2 tablespoons orange liqueur such as Grand Marnier or Cointreau

6 tablespoons water

1 (2-inch) sprig fresh rosemary

Juice from blood oranges (about ⅛ to ¼ cup)

Whipped Cream

3 cups heavy cream

3 tablespoons granulated sugar, or more to taste

Finishing Touches

24 ladyfingers, lightly toasted in the oven

1 cup toasted and chopped pistachios, or more if desired

GRAND MARNIER BLOOD ORANGE TART

This blood orange tart puts a new spin on the traditional orange tart you'll find in pastry shops all over France. If you really want to take it over the top, serve it with a bit of sauce on the side. A very dark chocolate sauce or a salted caramel sauce makes a great accompaniment and softens the edge of the orange flavor. Be prepared to do cartwheels!

Makes 1

Crust

2 cups unbleached all-purpose flour

½ teaspoon salt

1 teaspoon blood orange or lemon zest

½ cup confectioners' sugar

12 tablespoons cold unsalted butter, cut into pieces

1 egg

1 teaspoon Grand Marnier or other orange liqueur, if desired

Filling

¾ cup blood orange juice

1 teaspoon blood orange zest

¼ cup dark brown sugar

⅓ cup mascarpone cheese

3 large eggs plus 3 egg yolks

1 tablespoon Grand Marnier or other orange liqueur, if desired

Finishing Touches

2 blood oranges, peeled and sliced into rounds

Confectioners' sugar

Preheat oven to 375°F and position a rack in the center of the oven. Coat an 11-inch fluted tart pan with removable bottom with 2 teaspoons butter and set aside.

To make the crust, combine flour, salt, zest, and confectioners' sugar in a medium bowl. Cut in butter with two knives and mix until the mixture resembles coarse crumbles. Combine the egg and liqueur in a small bowl and add to the flour mixture. Using a fork, stir until the crumbles come together. Turn onto a lightly floured surface and knead until dough is formed. Shape into a flattened disk, wrap in plastic wrap, and transfer to the freezer for 15 minutes.

After the dough is chilled, place it on a floured surface and roll into a 13-inch round. Transfer dough to the prepared tart pan and ease dough into the edges and up the side of the pan. Trim off excess dough and place tart shell in the refrigerator for 30 minutes.

When chilled, prick it all over with a fork. Line the pastry with foil and fill with weights or beans. Bake the crust until the edges turn golden, approximately 15 minutes. Remove the weights and foil and bake 10 more minutes. Transfer pan to a rack to cool.

For the filling, combine blood orange juice, zest, brown sugar, and mascarpone in the bowl of a stand mixer fitted with a paddle attachment and beat until smooth. Add eggs and yolks one at a time, beating after each addition. Add liqueur and beat until smooth. Pour filling into tart shell. Bake until filling is lightly browned, approximately 25 minutes.

Garnish with blood oranges and dust with confectioners' sugar.

Italian Blood Orange Tart with Cardamom Pastry Cream

By now you know that cardamom is one of my very favorite aromatic spices. It combines brilliantly with the blood oranges, and the pistachios lend a sweet and nutty flavor.

Makes 1

Preheat oven to 375°F and position a rack in the center of the oven. Coat an 11-inch fluted tart pan with removable bottom with 2 teaspoons butter.

Combine flour, salt, zest, and confectioners' sugar in a medium bowl. Cut in butter with two knives and mix until the mixture resembles coarse crumbles. Combine egg and liqueur in a small bowl and add to the flour mixture. Using a fork, stir until it comes together. Turn onto a lightly floured surface and knead until dough is formed. Shape into a flattened disk, wrap in plastic wrap, and transfer to the freezer for 15 minutes.

After dough is chilled, place it on a floured surface and roll into a 13-inch round. Place dough in prepared tart pan and ease dough into the edges and up the side of the pan. Trim excess dough and refrigerate for 30 minutes.

Remove the tart shell from the refrigerator and prick it all over with a fork. Line with foil and fill with weights or beans. Bake until the edges turn golden, about 15 minutes. Remove the weights and foil, and bake 10 more minutes. Place pan on rack to cool.

For the pastry cream, heat milk, cream, and cardamom pods in a medium saucepan over medium heat to just below the boiling point. Remove from the heat, cover with a lid, and allow mixture to steep for 15 minutes. Pour through a fine-mesh strainer to remove cardamom. Return milk to saucepan and reheat to just below the boiling point. In a medium bowl, whisk together sugar, and cornstarch. When the milk is hot, pour about ½ cup of it into the cornstarch mixture and whisk to blend well. Pour this back into the saucepan and cook over medium heat, whisking constantly to prevent lumps, until it comes to a boil and thickens. ››

Crust

- **2 cups unbleached all-purpose flour**
- **½ teaspoon salt**
- **1 teaspoon blood orange zest**
- **½ cup confectioners' sugar**
- **12 tablespoons cold unsalted butter, cut into pieces**
- **1 egg**
- **1 teaspoon Grand Marnier or other orange liqueur, if desired**

Pastry Cream

- **1 cup whole milk**
- **½ cup heavy cream**
- **1 tablespoon cardamom pods, crushed slightly**
- **½ cup granulated sugar**
- **2 tablespoons cornstarch**
- **2 large eggs plus 2 large egg yolks**
- **3 tablespoons unsalted butter, cut into ½-inch pieces**
- **½ teaspoon pure vanilla extract ››**

Glaze

½ cup Blood Orange
    Marmalade (page 15)

2 teaspoons Grand Marnier
    or other orange liqueur,
    if desired

Whipped Cream

½ cup heavy cream

2 tablespoons granulated
    sugar

Finishing Touches

6 blood oranges, peeled and
    sliced into rounds

¾ cup toasted and chopped
    pistachios

« In a separate small bowl, whisk together eggs and yolks. Pour about ½ cup of the hot mixture into the eggs and whisk to blend thoroughly. Pour this mixture back into the saucepan and, stirring constantly over low heat, cook until it registers 170°F on an instant-read thermometer.

Remove pan from heat. Add butter and stir to blend it with custard. Pour the pastry cream through a fine-mesh strainer into a clean bowl and set the bowl into an ice bath. Place a piece of plastic wrap directly on the surface of the pastry cream to keep a skin from forming. Chill thoroughly.

Spread chilled pastry cream in the baked shell and chill for at least 1 hour.

To make the glaze, combine Blood Orange Marmalade and Grand Marnier, if desired, in a small bowl and brush over the chilled tart.

Next, make the whipped cream by first placing a metal mixing bowl and metal whisk in the freezer for 10 to 15 minutes. When chilled, place the heavy cream and sugar in the bowl. and whisk just until the cream reaches stiff peaks.

To finish, top tart with blood orange rounds, pistachios, and homemade whipped cream.

BLOOD ORANGE PANNA COTTA

We do a lot of entertaining, so when I plan my menus, which tend to include several courses (I love to cook for friends!), I like to include something light and sweet for dessert. My favorite dessert when entertaining is panna cotta, since it can be made ahead of time, and everyone seems to love it. Here's my favorite panna cotta recipe using blood orange juice.

Serves 6 to 8

Lightly coat 6 (8-ounce) or 8 (6-ounce) ramekins, custard cups, or baba molds with nonstick spray.

To make the panna cotta, place ½ cup milk in a small bowl. Sprinkle gelatin over the top, stirring to make sure all the granules are moistened. Set aside for at least 5 minutes.

Place remaining milk, cream, sugar, and cardamom seeds in a medium saucepan. Heat slowly just to the scalding point. Remove from the heat, cover with a lid, and allow mixture to steep for 15 minutes. When ready, remove the lid and add gelatin mixture to the pan, gently stirring to dissolve. Whisk in blood orange juice. Pour through a fine-mesh strainer into a container with a pour spout, and discard spices. Divide among the prepared cups or molds, cover, and place in the refrigerator to set, at least 3 to 4 hours.

To make the blood orange syrup, put all ingredients into a medium saucepan over low heat and stir until sugar dissolves. Increase heat and boil until reduced to 6 tablespoons. Strain into a small bowl and refrigerate.

To serve, dip each mold into hot water for a few seconds, just to loosen the panna cotta from the sides. Set a serving plate on top, flip over, and shake firmly until the panna cotta slides out onto the plate. Spoon blood orange syrup over each panna cotta.

Panna Cotta

1 cup whole milk, divided

2½ teaspoons powdered unflavored gelatin

1 cup heavy cream

½ cup granulated sugar

½ teaspoon cardamom seeds

¾ cup blood orange juice

Blood Orange Syrup

1⅓ cups blood orange juice

¼ cup granulated sugar

2 teaspoons blood orange zest

½ teaspoon ground cardamom

BLOOD ORANGE CHEESECAKE

Blood oranges and creamy mild cheeses make a happy coupling, and the ricotta cheese makes this a lighter cheesecake than most. I chose not to use sour cream in this recipe and replaced it with heavy whipped cream. The blood orange glaze is the crowning glory and adds a dark orange mirror-like top to this cheesecake.

Makes 1

Filling

2 cups ricotta cheese

Crust

1 cup crushed vanilla wafers

2 tablespoons granulated sugar

4 tablespoons melted salted or unsalted butter

Custard

3 tablespoons blood orange juice

1 envelope powdered unflavored gelatin

4 large egg yolks

½ cup plus 2 tablespoons whole milk

¾ cup granulated sugar

Pinch salt

1 teaspoon blood orange zest

1 teaspoon pure vanilla extract

4 ounces cream cheese

½ cup heavy cream, whipped

Blood Orange Glaze

½ cup blood orange juice, divided

¾ teaspoon powdered unflavored gelatin

2 tablespoons granulated sugar

¼ teaspoon cornstarch

Finishing Touch

2 blood oranges, peeled and sliced into rounds

Note: *Making this cheesecake is a 3-day process. First, the ricotta needs to drain overnight, then the cheesecake base needs to chill the second night before finishing up on the third day.*

To prepare the filling, place ricotta in a fine-mesh strainer lined with cheesecloth. Refrigerate several hours or overnight to drain ricotta.

Preheat oven to 325°F and position a rack in the center of the oven. Lightly spray or oil a 9-inch springform pan.

To make the crust, combine crumbs and sugar in a small bowl. Stir in melted butter with a fork until crumbs are moistened. Press into bottom of pan and bake for 10 minutes. »

‹‹ To make the custard, place blood orange juice in a small bowl. Sprinkle gelatin over the top, stirring to make sure all the granules are moistened. Set aside for 10 minutes to soften.

In a small heavy saucepan, beat egg yolks until smooth and whisk in milk. Gradually whisk in sugar and salt. Cook over low heat, stirring constantly, until the mixture coats the back of a spoon, about 7 minutes. (Do not allow to boil.)

Transfer to a bowl and stir in softened gelatin, blood orange zest, and vanilla, mixing until the gelatin is completely dissolved. Set aside.

Place drained ricotta in the bowl of a food processor and process until smooth. Add cream cheese and continue pulsing until smooth. With machine still running, add the warm custard and process just long enough to mix. Transfer mixture to a bowl and fold in the heavy whipped cream.

Pour mixture into prepared crust, cover with parchment or wax paper, and chill overnight.

To make the blood orange glaze, place 2 tablespoons blood orange juice in a small bowl and sprinkle gelatin over the surface. Set aside for 10 minutes to soften.

In a small saucepan, bring sugar and half of the juice to a boil. Combine remaining juice and cornstarch in a small bowl and stir until cornstarch dissolves. Whisk into the boiling blood orange juice. Remove from heat. Stir in softened gelatin. Cool until lukewarm or cool to touch.

To finish, pour cooled glaze over the top and garnish with blood orange rounds. Chill for 1 hour, the run a thin knife around the inside of the springform pan and transfer cheesecake to a serving plate.

BLOOD ORANGE MARMALADE MUFFINS

Flecks of blood orange zest from the marmalade are a deliciously hidden treasure in these aromatic muffins. You'll be craving them even before they are out of the oven. Enjoy these warm!

Makes 12

2 cups unbleached all-purpose flour

¼ cup granulated sugar

2 teaspoons baking powder

½ teaspoon baking soda

½ teaspoon salt

7 ounces almond paste (I use Odense brand)

½ cup blood orange juice

½ cup Blood Orange Marmalade (page 15)

4 tablespoons (½ stick) butter, melted

1 large egg

Preheat oven to 375°F and position a rack in the center of the oven. Lightly oil or spray a 12-cup muffin pan.

To make the batter, sift flour, sugar, baking powder, baking soda, and salt into a large bowl. Grate the almond paste into flour mixture. (The large-hole side of a box grater works well.) Mix grated almond paste into flour mixture until all pieces are coated. Separate any pieces that may have stuck together.

In a medium bowl, thoroughly combine blood orange juice, marmalade, melted butter, and egg until well combined. Make a well in the center of the flour mixture and pour in juice mixture. Beat quickly with a spoon until just combined. Spoon the batter into muffin pan.

Bake for 18 to 20 minutes, or until lightly golden on top. Serve with additional Blood Orange Marmalade on the side.

Blood Orange Sorbet with Rosemary

Serve this rosemary-infused sorbet as a palate cleanser at your next dinner party, or offer it up as dessert with simple shortbread cookies or crispy rolled wafers. Its ruby red-orange color is stunning and shows off well. Garnish with a rosemary sprig and a slice of blood orange for a lovely presentation.

Makes about 1 quart

Note: *If you have a frozen canister-style ice cream machine, allow 24 hours for the canister to freeze.*

In a medium saucepan, combine sugar and water. Place rosemary in a cheesecloth bag, add to the sugar water, and bring to a simmer. Continue simmering until the sugar dissolves and syrup thickens slightly, about 10 minutes. Remove from heat and steep for about 20 minutes. Discard rosemary and place syrup in refrigerator to chill.

To make the sorbet, combine blood orange juice with about 1 cup of rosemary syrup in a large bowl. Add liqueur and salt, pour into an ice cream maker, and freeze according to the manufacturer's instructions until frozen but still soft. Transfer it to a storage container, cover, and freeze until firm.

Simple Syrup
¾ cup granulated sugar

¾ cup water

2 to 3 sprigs fresh rosemary

Base
2 cups blood orange juice

2 tablespoons Cointreau, Grand Marnier, or other orange liqueur

Pinch salt

BLOOD ORANGE FROZEN YOGURT

Frozen yogurt is another smooth and creamy treat Americans have fallen head over heels for. This is a very simple recipe you can whip up in minutes. If it's for the kids, leave out the liqueur, but if it's for you, go ahead and indulge a bit.

Makes about 1 quart

2 cups blood orange juice

1 cup granulated sugar

4 cups plain or Greek-style yogurt

1 teaspoon grated blood orange zest, if desired

1 tablespoon Cointreau, Grand Marnier, or other orange liqueur, if desired

Note: *If you have a frozen canister-style ice cream machine, allow 24 hours for the canister to freeze.*

Thoroughly combine all ingredients except liqueur. Pour into an ice cream maker and freeze according to manufacturer's instructions. Just before the frozen yogurt completely solidifies, add the liqueur. Serve immediately or transfer it to a storage container, cover, and freeze until firm. Soften slightly before serving.

APPENDIX

In sixth grade Mrs. Walker
slapped the back of my head
and made me stand in the corner
for not knowing the difference
between *persimmon* and *precision.*
How to choose

persimmons. This is precision.
Ripe ones are soft and brown-
spotted.
Sniff the bottoms. The sweet one
will be fragrant. How to eat:
put the knife away, lay down
newspaper.
Peel the skin tenderly, not to tear
the meat.
Chew the skin, suck it,
and swallow. Now, eat
the meat of the fruit,
so sweet,
all of it, to the heart.

Donna undresses, her stomach is
white.
In the yard, dewy and shivering
with crickets, we lie naked,
face-up, face-down.
I teach her Chinese.
Crickets: *chiu chiu.* Dew: I've
forgotten.
Naked: I've forgotten.
Ni, wo: you and me.
I part her legs,
remember to tell her
she is beautiful as the moon.

Other words
that got me into trouble were
fight and *fright, wren* and *yarn.*
Fight was what I did when I was
frightened,
Fright was what I felt when I was
fighting.
Wrens are small, plain birds,

yarn is what one knits with.
Wrens are soft as yarn.
My mother made birds out of yarn.

I loved to watch her tie the stuff;
a bird, a rabbit, a wee man.

Mrs. Walker brought a persimmon
to class
and cut it up
so everyone could taste
a *Chinese apple.* Knowing
it wasn't ripe or sweet, I didn't eat
but watched the other faces.

My mother said every persimmon
has a sun
inside, something golden, glowing,
warm as my face.

Once, in the cellar, I found two
wrapped in newspaper,
forgotten and not yet ripe.
I took them and set both on my
bedroom windowsill,
where each morning a cardinal
sang, *The sun, the sun.*

Finally understanding
he was going blind,
my father sat up all one night

waiting for a song, a ghost.
I gave him the persimmons,
swelled, heavy as sadness,
and sweet as love.

This year, in the muddy lighting
of my parents' cellar, I rummage,
looking
for something I lost.
My father sits on the tired, wooden
stairs,
black cane between his knees,
hand over hand, gripping the
handle.
He's so happy that I've come home.
I ask how his eyes are, a stupid
question.
All gone, he answers.

Under some blankets, I find a box.
Inside the box I find three scrolls.
I sit beside him and untie
three paintings by my father:
Hibiscus leaf and a white flower.
Two cats preening.
Two persimmons, so full they want
to drop from the cloth.

He raises both hands to touch the
cloth,
asks, *Which is this?*

This is persimmons, Father.

*Oh, the feel of the wolftail on the
silk,
the strength, the tense
precision in the wrist.
I painted them hundreds of times
eyes closed. These I painted blind.
Some things never leave a person:
scent of the hair of one you love,
the texture of persimmons,
in your palm, the ripe weight.*

BECK GROVE & LA VIGNE ORGANICS

All fruits used in La Vigne products are grown at Beck Grove and all produce grown at Beck Grove is 100% organic as certified by the California Certified Organic Farmers Certification. Fresh fruit and products are available seasonally. www.lavignefruits.com or call 760.723.9997

FRESH 100% ORGANIC FRUIT, AVAILABLE ONLY IN SEASON

- Blood Oranges
- Fuyu Persimmons
- Kaffir Limes
- Kumquats
- Meyer Lemons
- Minneolas
- Navel Oranges
- Satsuma Tangerines

BLOOD ORANGE PRODUCTS

- **Blood Orange Juice**
  Refreshing and delicious.

- **Blood Orange Syrup**
  Features a distinctive blood orange flavor; use on pancakes, breakfast food, or as a topping for ice cream.

KUMQUAT PRODUCTS

- **Kumquat Fruit Leather**
  Tasty, chewy dried fruit treat.

- **Kumquat Conserve**
  Plump organic fruits delicious for breakfasts, desserts, and more.

- **Kumquat Ginger Syrup**
  Features a distinctive kumquat flavor; use on pancakes, breakfast food or as a topping for ice cream.

- **Kumquat Piquant Sauce**
  A distinctive condiment, dipping sauce, or marinade.

- **Kumquat Purée**

PERSIMMON PRODUCTS

- **Freeze-Dried Persimmons**
  A delightful snack that melts in your mouth.

- **Dried, Sliced Persimmons**
  A delicious, healthy snack.

- **Persimmon Chipotle Sauce**
  A distinctive condiment, dipping sauce, or marinade.

- **Persimmon Fruit Leather**
  Tasty, chewy dried fruit treat with a touch of ginger.

- **Persimmon Salad Dressing**
  Distinctive flavor inspires all types of salads and vegetables.

- **Persimmon Salsa**
  Try this in cooking, as a dipping sauce, or a marinade.

- **Persimmon Purée**

HERB PRODUCTS

- **Lemongrass Powder**
  Aromatic seasoning commonly used to enhance curry, soups, stews, and casseroles.

- **Dried Lemongrass**
  Makes a zesty, refreshing drink that is delicious hot or cold.

- **Fresh Lemongrass**
  Widely used in Thai and other Asian cuisines; makes a delicious tea.

- **Fresh Bay Leaves**
  Bay Leaves enhance the flavor of stews, soups, stocks, marinades, meat and fish dishes.

- **Dried Kaffir Lime Leaves**
Use as a seasoning or in hot tea.

- **Fresh Kaffir Lime Leaves**

- **Hoja Santos**
Popular Mexican herb. Large, aromatic, and green. Use for flavoring, as a wrap over savories, and in drinks.

- **Fresh Rosemary**

LEMON PRODUCT

- **Moroccan Lemon Preserves**
A traditional flavoring for Moroccan tagines, poultry, meat or seafood.

GOURMET DESSERTS

- **Kumquat Ginger Tea Bread**
Our delicious tea bread is mixed with just the right blend of sugar and spices, and then layered with kumquats, ginger pieces and walnuts.

- **Kumquat Ginger Cookies**
A gourmet cookie with a kumquat twist! Our Organic Kumquat Ginger Cookies are chock full of flavorful kumquats, walnuts with candied ginger too.

- **Kumquat Ginger Scones**
Treat yourself to a down home taste with a distinct kumquat flavor and a taste of perfection. Winner of "Best of Division" 2006 San Diego County Fair.

GIFT BASKETS & BAGS

Check our online store for current gift baskets and gift bags featuring fresh organic fruits, organic condiments, and gourmet desserts. www.lavignefruits.com

INDEX

Kumquat-Glazed Chicken with Bok Choy, 96
Kumquat-Marinated Chinese Chicken
   Pancakes, 91
Pork Loin with Rice Stuffing and Kumquat
   Glaze, 100
Portuguese Fuyu Persimmon Chicken, 39
Southwestern Chili with Blood Orange
   Sauce, 184
Tunisian Chicken Wings with Blood Oranges, 187

PASTA

Fuyu Persimmon Chipotle Risotto with
   Scallops, 31
Fuyu Persimmon Spiced Shrimp Noodles, 32
Kumquat Pasta with Hazelnuts, 103

PIE CRUSTS

Chocolate Cookie Pie Crust, 57
Gingersnap Pie Crust, 57
Graham Cracker Pie Crust, 57

PIES & TARTS

All Season Fuyu Persimmon, Blood Orange,
   and Pecan Pie, 58
Fuyu Persimmon Tarte Tatin, 62
Grand Marnier Blood Orange Tart, 200
Italian Blood Orange Tart with Cardamom
   Pastry Cream, 203
Kumquat Napoleon, 140
Layered Kumquat Supreme Pie, 132
Quick Kumquat Refrigerator Pie, 128
Triple Layer Fuyu Persimmon Pie, 54

SALADS

Beet Piquant Salad with Blood Oranges,
   Avocados, and Pistachios, 87
Blood Orange Salad with Candied
   Almonds, 175
Blood Orange Spinach Salad, 176
Blood Orange Tuna-Stuffed Cherry Pepper
   Salad, 180
Grilled Sirloin with Blood Oranges, Asiago,
   and Greens, 179

Kumquat Raspberry Layered Gel, 88
Scallop and Fennel Salad with Kumquat and
   Blood Orange Vinaigrette, 84

SEAFOOD

Blood Orange Tuna-Stuffed Cherry Pepper
   Salad, 180
Crab Cakes with Blood Oranges and Papaya
   Sauce, 191
Fuyu Persimmon Chipotle Risotto with
   Scallops, 31
Fuyu Persimmon Spiced Shrimp Noodles, 32
Grilled Lobster with Fuyu Persimmon Chipotle
   Sauce, 35
Lobster Corn Cakes with Blood Oranges and
   Avocados, 188
Mahi-Mahi with Blood Orange Salsa, 192
Mahi-Mahi Quesadilla with Fuyu Persimmon
   Salsa, 28
Moroccan Fish with Blood Oranges, 195
Scallop and Fennel Salad with Kumquat and
   Blood Orange Vinaigrette, 84

SOUPS

Cool Palate-Pleasing Fuyu Persimmon
   and Blood Orange Soup, 23
Chipotle Fuyu Persimmon and Pumpkin
   Soup, 24
Southwest Fuyu Persimmon and Roasted
   Red Pepper Soup, 27

TRIFLES, PUDDINGS & PANNA COTTA

Blood Orange Ladyfinger Trifle, 199
Blood Orange Panna Cotta, 207
Coconut Tapioca Pudding with Kumquat
   Ginger Syrup, 159
Fuyu Persimmon Panna Cotta, 73
Greek Yogurt Panna Cotta with Honeyed
   Kumquat Sauce, 164
Kumquat Blood Orange Ginger Parfait, 160
Kumquat Noodle Pudding (Kugel), 155
Kumquat Rice Pudding, 156